Hawks Aloft

THE STORY OF
HAWK MOUNTAIN

"Blind men! let the birds live in the woods and build and feed and sing and roam. Sluggards! spread the wings of your mind to the sky, and rise from the earth. Strive not to catch but to become birds!"—*Petrarch*.

Hawks Aloft

THE STORY OF HAWK MOUNTAIN

BY

Maurice Broun

STACKPOLE
BOOKS

Published by
STACKPOLE BOOKS
5067 Ritter Road
Mechanicsburg, PA 17055
www.stackpolebooks.com

Printed in the United States of America

Cover design by Wendy A. Reynolds
Cover illustration: red-tailed hawk by John W. Strawbridge

10 9 8 7 6 5 4 3 2 1

First edition

Library of Congress Cataloging-in-Publication Data
Broun, Maurice, 1906-1979.
    Hawks aloft: the story of Hawk Mountain / by Maurice
    Broun. —Anniversary ed.
        p. cm.
    ISBN 0-8117-2790-4 (alk. paper)
        1. Hawks—Pennsylvania—Hawk Mountain Sanctuary—
Anecdotes. 2. Birds, Protection of—Pennsylvania—Hawk
Mountain Sanctuary—Anecdotes. 3. Hawk Maountain Sanctuary
(Pa.)—Anecdotes. 4. Broun, Maurice, 1906-1979. I. Title.

QL696.F32 B74   2000
598.9'44'0974816—dc21

                                                    99-053516

To Edith McLellan Hale,

the "tall, gracious lady," mentioned on page 3, who encouraged a small boy in his quest of birds, this book is affectionately dedicated.

PREFACE TO THE MILLENNIAL EDITION

In celebrating this millennial edition of *Hawks Aloft*, there is no need to retell the story Maurice Broun so passionately and color-fully narrates in his remarkable book, now widely recognized as one of the conservation classics of the twentieth century. Nor is it necessary merely to add to the prefatory material so ably con-tributed to the previous editions by Roger Tory Peterson, Michael Harwood, and Joseph W. Taylor. That further preface to this classic risks dismissal as a pretext simply attests to the achievement of an ever-growing association of people motivated by the sublime *nat-ural* classic of migrating raptors and dedicated to a vision of keep-ing hawks aloft. Yet it is perhaps fitting, in giving lift to this edition, to consider a millennial preface for Hawk Mountain Sanctuary itself.

In the beginning, so Broun's story makes clear, there were but few faces involved. "Thinking like a mountain," Aldo Leopold's trope for salvation-through-wildness, required an enclosure for Broun. In his words it required a refuge "enclosed with a strand of wire" because "Pennsylvania hunters have learned to respect a wire." It required the right of sanctuary, a safe passage, and immu-nity from harm at a spot along Kittatinny Ridge where hawks were most vulnerable to being blasted out of the sky. His utmost priority was to stop the wholesale slaughter that took place for several months each autumn at what was effectively the North Shootout.

This kind of intervention existed as a possibility in a country whose laws were based on a strong tradition of property rights. Ac-tualizing this possibility, the Emergency Conservation Committee, a group of New York City activists headed by Rosalie Edge, ob-tained a lease on some 1400 acres in 1934 and secured clear title in 1938, deeding it that year to the newly incorporated Hawk Moun-tain Sanctuary Association. The strategy pursued by the Commit-tee in obtaining title to Blue Mountain in order to control and su-pervise its use for the sake of wildlife would become the informing principle of The Nature Conservancy, an organization not estab-lished until 1946.

Over the years the Sanctuary has nearly doubled in size, and Hawk Mountain has become multifaceted—so much so that today "thinking like a mountain" involves a multiplicity of commitments, as well as an intertwining of conflicting strands of feeling, of reasoning, and of knowing. The "Hawk Mountain family" unto which Michael Harwood "gratefully"—and, I might add, touchingly—subscribed himself is not unlike any other expanding family in this regard. This is understandable, for it is but one of the consequences of our success, just one of the results of more than a million visitors having "taken home," as Joe Taylor put it, "our message about the value of raptors in the environment."

But in the wake of this success, what now is Hawk Mountain for? How do we best press the case for the value of raptors into the next century? In thinking about this we might return to one of Broun's most philosophical chapters, "Sanctuary—We Mean It!" "Sanctuary," for Broun, implied a "pact with nature." This pact was to be honored on the principle that "all wildlife is inviolate." The implications were as clear as could be for wildlife management: "stringent protection of the wildlife, and letting nature alone to work out her own checks and balances." If Broun found it necessary to "restrict in numbers" the black rat snake, this only demonstrated that some interventions in a sanctuary were acceptable. For Maurice Broun "sanctuary" was never a "pure" place.

What is noteworthy about Broun's thinking is that his understanding of *sanctuary* entangles two concepts. One is land-based, that of a physical place, and is directed by the notion that nature knows best. This enclosure concept provides permanent protection for all wildlife contained within its bounds by permitting nature to reign. This paradisiacal notion has its origins in the first garden. Human tampering is seen as interference. Its range runs from an entire ecosystem to a small, fragmented patch or woodlot, a pond we treasured growing up, nothing even as large as Broun's Boston Public Garden. The heart makes places sacred too. We all know this, and those who have grown up under the tutelage of the Mountain have sanctified a place the rest of us have come merely to love.

The other concept underlying Broun's *sanctuary* is that of temporary protection from harm during flight or exodus. This is the notion of "sanctuary" invoked when Broun calls Hawk Mountain "the world's first sanctuary for the birds of prey." This concept is directed by the notion that human beings know best. Conservationists save by intervening—here, in the misguided behavior of gunners. The spectacle value of North Lookout resides in the physiography of the Kittatinny—a major leading line—that, in combination with westerly and northerly winds, makes the Lookout an ideal concentration point from which to view these masters of the sky shooting past. As individuals, most are present within our airspace for no more than several minutes each year. Even as populations and species, they are present for little more than a few months. These raptors don't reside at Hawk Mountain. They benefit from safe passage.

Thrilling thousands of visitors who stand in awe of their annual flight, they benefit indirectly from the raptor conservation programs conducted under the auspices of Hawk Mountain and supported by its enlightened members. This indirect vantage is acknowledged in conceiving of the Sanctuary as a "school in the clouds." What began by securing a rocky outcrop has become a celebration of migration and a challenging opportunity to expand our reach. After all, the outlook for the century ahead is alarming. We live increasingly in a world of natural fragments. The need now for a deeper and more comprehensive understanding of the interrelation between nature and culture is pronounced. The "pact" that Broun's sanctuary implied has ceased to be an implication for us. We have begun, as conservation biologists today invite all to do, to think differently. We require a new pact.

Sanctuaries and refuges are small tracts, fragments of land, rather than national parks or wilderness reserves. The scale is vastly different, and considerations of scale are important. Scale has implications for a sanctuary's viability as a nature reserve, for its ability to preserve biodiversity. Hawk Mountain is a point along a corridor in the sky. As a piece of Appalachia our small Sanctuary is much more like a buffer zone, in its use and in its possibilities, than any core area. The pact Broun made with nature at Hawk Mountain today prescribes behavior toward core areas, not buffers. Buffers permit regulated visitation and on-site research and education activities, as well as pastoral retreat.

Can we think bigger than a mountain? We have begun to do so by recognizing and reaffirming our origins. This means letting go of Broun's insupportable notion of countless small sanctuaries as repositories of "all types of ecological niches" and, rather, coming to protect hawk passage throughout the world by teaching others to replicate our local efforts in other corridors, as well as by carefully monitoring and controlling the continued use of our site. More interventions are needed today in order to accomplish the possible.

By changing the recreational behavior along the Kittatinny Corridor—from hawk-shoot to hawk-watch—conservationists managed to secure an aerodynamically vital pass on Endless Mountain. Roger Tory Peterson refers to Blue Mountain as a "migratory highway," but his metaphor conceals the fact that ours is but one passageway on the route. The road is long and networked. It may well be that at the time Peterson wrote Broun indeed had claim to "the distinction of having seen more birds of prey than any other man living," but we are living in a different world. Now a visitor to Veracruz, thanks in part to the efforts of the Mountain, can, with fortuitous timing, see more birds of prey in a day than "the Hawk Man" saw in a lifetime.

The Sanctuary's River of Rocks has led to Mexico's River of Raptors, and this "river" stretches from North America south through the land funnel of Middle America into the spreading South American continent. Our international initiatives have carried us from "Hawks Aloft" to "Hawks Aloft Worldwide," the Sanctuary's collaborative effort to atlas raptor migration globally. These leading-line efforts, along with our Internship Program and our Center for Conservation Learning, exemplify our direction for the next century. Hawk Mountain is for sanctuaries as corridors proliferating worldwide so that raptors survive the next millennium. The Mountain is for sanctuaries as salvaged fragments to be studied for their diminishing biodiversity. That is what we mean by sanctuary. The heroic story reissued in this expanded edition was achieved by thinking like a mountain. For an expansive sequel to our hard-won success, we will need to start thinking like continents.

JOHN ROWLETT
Chair, Education Committee
Hawk Mountain Sanctuary Association
Board of Directors
2000

PREFACE TO THE FIFTIETH ANNIVERSARY EDITION

This wonderful book reverberates with the excitement of the pioneer days of Hawk Mountain Sanctuary. Old-time conservationists know the basic story well: In the early 1930s Rosalie Barrow Edge, the strong-minded organizer of a group called the Emergency Conservation Committee, learned that hunters climbed Hawk Mountain every fall to shoot hawks migrating along the Kittatinny Ridge. The hawks — then unprotected by law — were being killed by the hundreds and thousands each year, and many of them suffered lingering deaths on the stony slopes below the shooting stands. Mrs. Edge arranged to lease the mountain and then to buy it, and she hired Maurice Broun as the first warden in 1934. What happened next — between 1934 and 1948 — is the subject of *Hawks Aloft*. Maurice's spirited tales of the early trials and victories at Hawk Mountain make this a classic document in the history of the conservation movement.

Beginning with those years, Hawk Mountain Sanctuary has exerted a strong influence on raptor conservation in the United States and abroad, by both example and education. Visitors have come to the mountain from short and great distances, and many have taken home our message about the value of raptors in the environment, helping — among other things — to spur local and national legislation to protect birds of prey. Maurice began this work at his "School in the Clouds," which he talks about in *Hawks Aloft*.

The sanctuary has also had a major influence on knowledge about North American raptors. Maurice's observations of the autumn migrations of birds of prey, published in *Hawks Aloft* and in scientific journals and popular magazines during the 32 years he was warden and curator here, combined with the observations published by his successors, have had profound effects. First, before the sanctuary was founded virtually no one except the hawk-shooters knew there were places where birds of prey concentrated on migration. So Maurice and Hawk Mountain introduced bird-lovers to a great and beautiful spectacle. Next, observations recorded each year from the mountain lookouts have taught ornithologists important things about the ranges and migratory behavior of northeastern birds of prey.

We've been making daily counts of migrating raptors (and other birds) from the lookouts since 1934, and we've been recording their passage by the *hour* since the 1960s. In his foreword, which you'll find a few pages farther on, Maurice told an anecdote about a woman who visited the North Lookout one fall day in the '40s and watched the hawkwatchers with amazement as they enthusiastically kept the day's count of passing hawks. "Poor people," the lady said to her companion; "simple, aren't they, counting birds?" But that "simple" activity not only increased understanding of north-eastern raptors; it eventually became the foundation for a serious, ambitious, complex, continent-wide research project. Hundreds of mostly amateur ornithologists, "hooked on hawks" by the migratory spectacle first popularized at Hawk Mountain, now make hour-by-hour hawk-counts at many places during spring and fall migrations and pool their data in efforts to improve our understanding of the movements of raptors across all of North America. The participants, organized by the Hawk Migration Association of North America (now ten years old), haven't perfected the approach yet, but they've come a long way, and we have high hopes that the same sort of organization and enthusiasm generated in this cooperative data-gathering can be applied to solving other questions in North American ornithology.

So the flame first lit and held aloft by Rosalie Edge and Maurice Broun goes on casting light into dark corners. As we celebrate the

Sanctuary's semicentennial anniversary our commitment to raptor-conservation remains as passionate as the commitment of the pioneers, and we hope that our contributions to ornithological knowledge will from time to time be as revolutionary as those of Maurice Broun during the era he described in *Hawks Aloft*.

JOSEPH W. TAYLOR
President, Hawk Mountain
Sanctuary Association
1984

PREFACE TO THE MEMORIAL EDITION

After Maurice Broun died in the autumn of 1979, many of his friends gathered at the chapel of Muhlenberg College in Allentown, Pennsylvania, for a service celebrating the life of this extraordinary conservation pioneer. To perpetuate that spirit of celebration this new edition of Maurice's classic, *Hawks Aloft,* is being issued by the Hawk Mountain Sanctuary Association. As "managing editor" of the edition I would like to acknowledge with gratitude the assistance of the sanctuary staff, Dodd, Mead and Company, *Defenders* magazine, the photographer Cameron Davidson, and Irma Broun.

Maurice Broun was one of the major figures of his generation in the field of conservation. His most important contribution spanned 32 years, 1934 to 1966, when he served as curator of Hawk Mountain Sanctuary. *Hawks Aloft* covers the early years of that adventure.

The book does not say much about Maurice's life before he came to Pennsylvania. He was born in New York City in 1906, the son of Roumanian immigrants who died when he was still an infant. He spent his childhood in the homes of relatives, in an orphanage, and in foster homes. By the time he was 13 he was living, not happily, with a foster family in Boston. That spring he experienced his "conversion" to ornithology — an incident he relates early in this book. At 15 he left home, and to support himself while he finished high school he worked as a busboy and worked in a hospital laundry. Meanwhile, he quickly built a reputation as a bright, enthusiastic young birder. He led bird walks in the Boston Public Garden near his rented room and published a pamphlet on the birds found there.

After graduation from high school he got a job as a bellhop at the Women's City Club of Boston. But after a few years, by the best of good fortune, he was hired by the state ornithologist, Edward Howe Forbush, to help produce the final volume of *The Birds of Massachusetts and Other New England States,* which Forbush was preparing with his colleague John B. May. Those two deans of North American ornithology were clearly impressed by the abilities and character of their assistant, and they helped propel Maurice into a life of conservation work.

First he went to Lenox, Massachusetts, where he developed the Pleasant Valley Bird Sanctuary. Then he was hired as research associate at the Austin Ornithological Research Station on Cape Cod; during that stint he met and courted his wife, Irma Penniman — a romance he describes with grace and tenderness in *Hawks Aloft.* Next, he went to work as staff naturalist for the Treadway Inns, building trails and a nature center in the Adirondacks and the Berkshires. And then he and Irma came to Hawk Mountain.

In 1966 Maurice Broun retired as curator. He had made such a success of Hawk Mountain Sanctuary that crowd-control was becoming a pressing problem, and he did not enjoy that. So he accepted an "emeritus" tacked after "curator", and he and Irma moved to a farm one ridge away. They called the place Strawberry Hill. There Maurice created a new nature sanctuary — for himself and Irma and the many friends and student groups who often descended on them. He was full of honors — author of many ornithological notes and articles and his *Index to North American Ferns* as well as *Hawks Aloft,* recipient of honorary degrees. And in the 1970s the generation of hawk-migration students who had grown up at his knee, so to speak, astonished him by developing a continental network of hawkwatches for migration study and then acknowledging him as the father of it all.

Astonishment. If anything about Maurice Broun's character

sticks in memory it is his perpetual capacity to be astonished, to be moved. He was able to experience those lovely small moments that come to an open-eyed naturalist — a new bird in the garden hedge, or a red-tailed hawk, wings half closed, scooting down the sky, or warblers bathing in a mountaintop puddle — and not be embarrassed by the charge of joy that compelled him to turn to his companions and say, "Isn't this *amazing?"*

Maurice was restless and feisty — always on the alert for the good to be done and the bad to be opposed. He was not the sort of man one liked to find on the opposite side of any argument, because he was persistent, informed and eloquent. He was a first-rate teacher and played a major part in making hawk-protection respectable and, at last, successful.

I began visiting Hawk Mountain in the 1960s, which makes me a late-comer. But it seems to me that — aside from the obvious role of protecting birds of prey — the most important characteristic of Hawk Mountain Sanctuary was and is the spirit of Family that has pervaded the place. *Hawks Aloft* is chock-full of this family. Over the years hundreds, probably thousands, of sanctuary members have become so convinced of the rightness of the sanctuary's message and mission that they have given it far more than their annual dues. They have come to the mountain to invest time and much energy in a piece of earth, rocks, trees, ferns, wildflowers, insects, reptiles, mammals, birds, and in each other. And so I gratefully subscribe myself — member of the Hawk Mountain family, Maurice Broun *paterfamilias,*

MICHAEL HARWOOD
1980

INTRODUCTION TO THE FIRST EDITION

Every week end from mid-September, just before the mass exodus of the broad-winged hawks, to early November, when the last of the red-tails drifts through, hundreds of nature-minded motorists converge on the Blue Mountain near Hamburg in eastern Pennsylvania to watch one of the most dramatic shows on earth. There, among the watchers who have climbed the trail to the bald peak with its tumbled boulders of Tuscarora sandstone, stands Maurice Broun, the "Hawk Man of Hawk Mountain." Broun probably has the distinction of having seen more birds of prey than any other man living.

When I first met Maurice Broun nearly twenty years ago he was busily banding birds at the Austin Station on the outer arm of Cape Cod. Later I found him directing the nature activities at Long Trail Lodge in the heart of the Green Mountains of Vermont. He has always preferred to live and work in such places. He is not an armchair naturalist. Now at "Schaumboch's," the little white house far up on the side of Hawk Mountain, he has found the one place on earth that best suits his Thoreauvian tastes. It is a far cry from the streets of Boston where one day, long ago, he sought escape from the artificiality of the city in the Public Garden, and first discovered the birds.

For years many of us have hoped that Maurice Broun would put this story, as well as some of his knowledge of hawks, between covers. This he has done, recounting the earlier history of the mountain, when the passing raptores were ambushed by a waiting army deployed across the rocky summit; and how the Hawk Mountain Sanctuary Association, under the banner of the militant conservationist, Mrs. Rosalie Edge, purchased the mountain and established the world's first hawk sanctuary, one of the first real breaks the hawks have ever had. He analyzes the factors that make the Blue Mountain a migratory highway, and tells of the red-letter days when the great flights came through. But Broun is as interested in people as he is in birds, so this book is also a human-interest story. In addition to the tale of how he and his vivacious wife Irma set up housekeeping on the mountain, he describes his Pennsylvania Dutch neighbors with their old-world ways, and the procession of interesting people who have swarmed in from more than forty states to watch the pageant in the sky.

When the cool drafts from the Northwest add finis to summer and the first frosts turn the green of the countryside to red and gold, the time has come to grasp the steering wheel and head for this bird watcher's mecca. "Going to Hawk Mountain" is now a tradition to thousands who live within a day's drive. Many bird clubs as far away as Ohio, New York State, and the District of Columbia, make a yearly pilgrimage. On the mountaintop I can always count on seeing many old acquaintances from distant cities, not to mention my old friends, the hawks.

Today we know how important the hawks and other predators are to the natural balance, guardians, as it were, of the health and vigor of the outdoor world. The epic of Hawk Mountain has done more than anything else to publicize the cause of hawk preservation. Like the drama of the egrets, it is one of the great heart-warming stories of bird conservation.

ROGER TORY PETERSON

ACKNOWLEDGMENTS

The chapter on the Golden Eagle is reprinted with the kind permission of *Nature Magazine*. Chapter 9—"The Ghosts of Schaumboch's" appeared originally in pamphlet form, published by the Hawk Mountain Sanctuary Association. A few paragraphs have appeared in *The Auk* (Journal of the American Ornithologists' Union), and some material has been adapted from the Sanctuary *Newsletters*. Thanks are due Miss Edith Patterson and to Mrs. Frederick S. Luden for their help in obtaining historical data; to Dr. Francis J. Trembley and to Dr. Lawrence Whitcomb, both of Lehigh University, for suggestions and reading certain parts of the book; and to Raymond T. Bond of Dodd, Mead and Company, for numerous suggestions for improvement of the manuscript. I am deeply grateful to Mrs. Charles Noel Edge for her valued and critical reading of several chapters, and to my wife who has helped me in more ways than I can tell. Finally, I wish to thank all the loyal friends and devotees of the Sanctuary, without whose interest and encouragement this book could never have been birthed.

MAURICE BROUN

May 1, 1949

FURTHER ACKNOWLEDGMENTS

We owe the inclusion of the many wonderful photographs for this millennial edition of *Hawks Aloft* to many people, most of all Maurice Broun. I would like to especially give credit to the efforts of volunteer Joseph A. Snook, who painstakingly copied archival prints for the Sanctuary's 50th anniversary in 1984. I am also grateful to the Julian W. Hill Archives and Library Endowment of Hawk Mountain, which has provided funds to copy additional archival prints, and to conserve our photographic treasures for time to come.

CYNTHIA LENHART
Executive Director
Hawk Mountain Sanctuary Association
2000

FOREWORD

We had been counting the oncoming red-tails and other hawks one exciting Sunday afternoon a few years ago. One after another the birds drifted past the Lookout in their effortless fashion, putting on a first-rate show for all interested spectators, of whom there were many, some wrapt in wonder at the spectacle, others seriously studying each passing bird, jotting figures into note-books. Everyone seemed to be enjoying the occasion—everyone, that is, except a stiff and sober middle-aged couple who regarded *us*, not the birds, with wonder. I saw the woman tap her finger to her head significantly, as she said to her escort: "Poor people; simple, aren't they, counting birds!" I felt like saying: "Don't waste your sympathy, lady; we're happy. I think we should be feeling sorry for *you*."

Poor, simple people, counting birds! The pity that there are not many more such harmless souls. Who ever heard of a bird-watcher inciting political rebellion (except Thoreau!), or committing murder or mayhem, or coveting his neighbor's house or his neighbor's wife! Show me the birdlover who has not a deep-rooted sense of humaneness. The concept of humaneness, as a basic part of one's social attitudes, is what is needed so desperately for the youths of our land, if we are to guide them along the road to true conservation ideals and practices.

Never was there a more dubious project than ours at Hawk Mountain. In the beginning, it looked like an utterly hopeless, thankless task. For the real protectionists, the voices that rang out boldly in defence of the persecuted birds of prey, rarely made any notable contribution towards the preservation of these birds. To whom could we turn for help —so sorely needed? We were unduly pessimistic. The response of warm-hearted, sympathetic people has been overwhelming. What was once the secret monopoly of a small local faction of hunters is now pridefully referred to by Hawk Mountain devotees who are scattered throughout the United States, and Canada, and elsewhere.

For the Sanctuary has been a source of great pleasure, and a wellspring of inspiration, to a large number of, shall we say "simple" people. Birds, and the solace they could bring, was what brought a mother and her husband to Hawk Mountain when they were in great anxiety about their son. She wrote to us: "The reason we went to Hawk Mountain was to keep us from going off the deep end . . . We started straight for Hawk Mountain as fast as we could go. I'm glad we went, for looking at the birds made life a little easier to bear."

Ernest C. Baker, a busy accountant, who has spent many a Sunday and Thanksgiving Day forenoon at the Sanctuary, wrote to me: "Hawk Mountain is always for me a place of retreat from a too-practical world. It is good for the soul to spend a few quiet hours there. . . ."

One fall a man from nearby Reading came on nearly every week end throughout the season, and even on occasional weekdays. He was under the stress of great responsibility, and his wife told Mrs. Edge that she did not know how he could have solved his problems which he did successfully, had it not been for the days spent on Hawk Mountain.

Some of the finest testimonials of the worth and significance of Hawk Mountain came to us during the war years. A member of the Army Air Forces sent these nostalgic words to Mrs. Edge: "I haven't the remotest chance of visiting the Sanctuary this year. To me Hawk Mountain is like a fever. I catch it with the first touch of cool weather, and it keeps burning in me right up until December." And another wrote: "Today I received the Newsletter, and believe me, it sure sent pangs through me. A dose of good clean mountain air, and the sight of the hawks winging by, can do more good than all the USO and Stage Door Canteens rolled into one."

Peter K. Dufault, another pilot in the Air Forces, forwarded the following message, expressing eloquently the rare spirit of fellowship one finds among true Hawk Mountaineers: "When I was at Harvard, I sought to find an organization of students and professors whose common interest was poetry. There were all kinds of literary clubs and societies there, of course, but somehow I couldn't find the right one. I was never very happy at the reunions I'd attend there. I think now I was looking for a group of people not so much interested in poetry as being poets themselves.

"When I think of the brief two days I spent at Hawk Mountain, it occurs to me that those few people up there on the ridge, drinking the coldness, and the rush of grey winds and the great sweep of sky—that *those* people were *my* kind. I don't remember the names of any of the watchers that were there when I was. But I would be glad if you will relay my greetings to such as are there, now.

"I cannot go there now; I may never get back there. So tell them to stand clear in the cold wind *for me*—till the wind-tears stream on their cheeks, to feel the unutterable sad rapture at those dark wings, arrowing out of the north and out of sight forever. Tell them to stand there in the mountain till the autumn sinks into their souls for good; till they find with a thrill of learning and a twinge of sorrow, what I found there, and will not forget."

Ben Goodwin, also an aviator, cooperated with me in our flight-speed experiments during the autumn of 1942. He wrote to Irma a few weeks before his death in a plane crash: "Those months I spent at Hawk Mountain were fruitful in more than scientific data. They gave me a 'back-log' of inspiration and strength to use when the going was rough. 'I will lift up mine eyes to the hills from whence cometh my strength.' I have needed that strength more than once, and at times when there were no hills, I recalled Hawk Mountain in the splendor of autumn.

"Three things with me are synonymous with Hawk Mountain—peace and quiet, good fellowship, and Irma Broun's apple pie."

The first breath of spring that comes to Hawk Mountain each year is a note like the following: "The Friendly Bird Club of Grade 6, Alexander Hamilton School (Morristown, N. J.) enclose in this letter a contribution to the good work of Hawk Mountain Sanctuary. . . . We have been studying the hawks and owls and are so glad to know that there is one place where these valuable birds are safe."

And from the Province of Quebec Society for the Protection of Birds, came another warm expression: "At a recent meeting of the Board of Directors of this Society it was decided that a donation . . . be made to your Association in appreciation of the good work it is doing for the protection of birds and wild life generally, and in furtherance of the aims of your organization." Our mailbox often holds letters like this, coming from Arizona, Oregon, Illinois, and England!

And if I may quote one last letter, from Mrs. S. R. Taber, of Philadelphia: "One of the best thrills of the early New Year is the receipt of your stirring Newsletter, even better than a flower catalogue, beloved as that is. The success you are making is perfectly grand. It lifts my spirits unbelievably! As an aged cripple I shall never see the Sanctuary, but I do rejoice in knowing how it is entering the lives of others."

These represent some of the "simple people" who have shared in the Hawk Mountain adventure—wonderful people who, in their keen enjoyment of hawks aloft have been as much a stimulus and an inspiration to us as the fascinating pageant of the hawks.

CONTENTS

Part One

Part Two

Part Three

PART ONE

"For who that has ever looked at nature in other regions, where this perpetual hideous war of extermination against all noble feathered life is not carried on, does not miss the great soaring bird in the scene—eagle, or vulture, or buzzard, or kite, or harrier—floating at ease on broad vans, or rising heavenwards in vast and ever-vaster circles?"—W. H. HUDSON

CHAPTER 1

SHAMBLES
TO SANCTUARY

My interest in birds was awakened one glorious, never-to-be forgotten morning in May when I was thirteen years of age. I had wandered into the Boston Public Garden and had come upon a group of serious-looking grown-ups scanning the treetops with field glasses. I looked on with open-eyed wonder, when a tall, gracious lady left the group and offered me her glasses; and presently I too was straining my neck upwards, looking at a dainty bird flitting nervously through the upper reaches of a willow tree. The bird, I was told, was a magnolia warbler. So graceful, so vivacious, so trim in its brilliant spring plumage of bright yellow, black and white, it was truly the most strikingly beautiful thing my eyes had ever beheld. A magnolia warbler! It had a *name*, which fell like music on my ears, accustomed only, as they were, to the strident sounds of the city streets. Birds suddenly became a daily excitement to me, a passion, and contact with birds in one way or another became as necessary to me as food.

I grew up in the heart of Boston—a poor environment, perhaps, for anyone to cultivate a love for wild birds. But I was fortunate. I met many friendly expert and amateur bird students in the city park, and all were helpful and encouraging to the small boy consumed with the bird passion. Within five years, with borrowed binoculars and books, I had learned and identified more than two hundred kinds of birds within five miles of the State House. And then my career with birds really began with a research job in the State House, in the Department of Agriculture, under two master bird men: Edward Howe Forbush, dean of American ornithologists, who for forty years, until his death in 1929, had been the State Ornithologist of Massachusetts; and his assistant, Dr. John B. May. It was a privilege to be associated with these men, both of whom were a tremendous stimulus and an inspiration to me. I helped Mr. Forbush for three years in the compilation of his monumental *Birds of Massachusetts and Other New England States.*

Dr. May was an authority on hawks. He understood hawks better than anyone else I knew. Perhaps it was my daily contact with Dr. May that crystallized my interest in hawks. In any event, the occasional hawks that I was fortunate to see in and around the outskirts of the city quickened my blood "like fiercely ringing bells or far-off bugles."

I learned with pain that not everyone felt about hawks as I did. My sentiments were akin to Thoreau's, who wrote "I would rather never taste chickens' meat nor hens' eggs than never to see a hawk sailing through the upper air again. This sight is worth incomparably more than chicken soup or a boiled egg." But mankind in general seemed bent on the extinction of the birds of prey, whose depredations on game birds could never be compared with the depredations of man himself.

Then, late in 1932, I learned about the graveyard of hawks at Drehersville, in east-central Pennsylvania. At that time I was a research associate at the Austin Ornithological Research Station, on Cape Cod. A fresh copy of *Bird Lore* on my desk carried the shocking intelligence in a few words, signed by Richard H. Pough: "On top of Blue Mountain above Drehersville, Schuylkill County, an appalling slaughter is going on. . . . Blue Mountain is a long, continuous ridge along which thousands of hawks pass in migration. First the broad-wings in September, and out of this flight I would say 60 were shot. Then came the sharp-shinned and Cooper's hawks—thousands of these were killed. The enclosed photographs show 218 birds picked up in about an hour last Sunday morning at one stand. Among others I have found 5 ospreys, a protected bird, of course, but one that will be shot every time, along with eagles, sparrow hawks, flickers, blue jays, so long as hawk-shooting of this sort is permitted. When 100 or 150 men, armed with pump guns, automatics, and double-barreled shotguns are sitting on top of a mountain looking for a target, no bird is safe. The birds are seldom retrieved, and I have found many wounded birds, some alive after several days."

I turned to my co-worker, Seth Low, who had also been jolted by this statement. We discussed the plight of our hawks, for great had been the depletion of their ranks through persistent persecution. Hawk-shooting campaigns were being urged by trigger-happy sportsmen throughout the country, reacting to propaganda to annihilate our hawks and owls issued by gun and ammunition makers.

Dr. Witmer Stone, ten years earlier, had called attention to the great destruction of migrating hawks by hunters at Cape May, New Jersey. And now we learned of the hideous mass murder of these noble birds in Pennsylvania, which must in itself have been an important factor in their decrease.

To a young conservationist, deeply sensitive to the value and the beauty of our native hawks, *Bird Lore's* fragmentary picture of carnage was profoundly shocking. And the worst of it was, I thought, that little if anything could be done to stop that slaughter, since Pennsylvania laws at that time provided merely nominal protection to but three kinds of hawks: the osprey, the bald eagle and the sparrow hawk.

How in the name of decency could this sort of thing be tolerated? Were there no merciful people in Pennsylvania capable of rallying support and militant action to wipe out this shambles? Little did I realize that within two years something would indeed be done about it; something would be done so effectively that for the first time in sixty-five years or more every migrating hawk would cross the mountain unmolested. And little did I dream that the strange pull of destiny was to draw me to Drehersville, that I would be granted a role in bringing about the metamorphosis of shambles into sanctuary.

Until recent years the extensive fall migrations of hawks and eagles along the Kittatinny Ridge were almost unknown to ornithologists. This is remarkable, for the flyway begins but a few miles above New York City. I say "almost unknown" because of a notable exception. The ancient flyway for the birds of prey was familiar to the late Dr. Waldron DeWitt Miller, of the American Museum of Natural History. From time to time Dr. Miller received a parcel of hawk skins for the Museum, from his friend Justus Von Lengerke, whose favorite pastime was hawk-shooting from a strategic stand in the Kittatinny Ridge of northern New Jersey. Von Lengerke, who was something of an ornithologist, enjoyed his sport for many years, and his kill must have been enormous. He died in 1929.

Von Lengerke had no monopoly on this sport. The Kittatinny Ridge, with a maximum elevation of two thousand feet, extends in unbroken relief from southeastern New York southwest across five states, and elsewhere along the ridge groups of men sought out favorable spots to kill the migrating hawks. By far the most popular, and most infamous, shooting grounds were located on a spur of the ridge, above Drehersville.

The topography of this ridge (designated as Blue Mountain on U. S. topographic maps) must be understood if we are to appreciate this concentration point of hawks and eagles. The long ridge, along which the hawks fly southward with a minimum of effort, riding the ascending air currents, here narrows to a slender bottleneck: a focal point for all migrating hawks. The razor-back ridge ends abruptly; its wooded slopes merge into a broad cross-ridge which zigzags southward. Jutting conspicuously from the trees of the cross-ridge are a series of promontories, in the line of flight of the migrating birds, affording a wide sweep of view down the valleys and across the ridges. A road winds up from Drehersville, crossing the broad cross-ridge. Every fall, for more years than most local residents could remember, hunters gravitated to this place in the mountains to enjoy a witch's holiday. As many as one hundred fifty to four hundred hunters swarmed over the mountain "lookouts" on a Sunday, and perhaps half as many were on hand during week days. Some of the hunters came from points sixty to a hundred miles distant, so attractive was this "sport" to the hunting fraternity.

The hawk-shoots had long been known to the Pennsylvania Game Commission. The Game Commission apparently favored the killing. In the early '20's the hawks had one articulate friend, the Honorable Henry W. Shoemaker. He tried to induce the Game Commission to put an end to the shooting but his efforts were fruitless. The Game Commission was responsible, in 1929, for legislation placing a five-dollar bounty on goshawks, a hawk that is rare in Pennsylvania. Not one hunter in a hundred would know a goshawk if he should ever see one. A goshawk bounty is really an incentive to kill all hawks, with the agreeable feature that the state has to pay the bounty only on goshawks.

In October, 1927, Dr. George M. Sutton, then connected with the Game Commission, visited the mountain to see for himself. He gathered up 158 hawks of four species, all killed by several gunners "in a remarkably short time." Dr. Sutton published a paper on plumage differences and other technical data, based on this collection of birds; it appeared in the *Wilson Bulletin,* 1928. Science was served. But no crusader aroused the sentiments of people who might be humanely disposed toward the birds.

Meanwhile the "hawk-shoots" were being well advertised in local newspapers. A typical example follows, quoted from the *Pottsville Journal* of late October, 1929: "SPORTSMEN SHOOT MIGRATING HAWKS. Pottsville Hunters Knock Down Pests from Point of Vantage in Blue Mountains. Kill 300 in single day.

"Thousands of huge hawks, redtails, marsh and goshawks, borne by a stiff northwest wind over a steep pinnacle in the Blue Mountains . . . are daily challenging hunters and sportsmen of Pottsville and vicinity.

"Chilled by the early October winds, many thousand hawks are sweeping past the mountain pinnacle, inviting extermination, a challenge that has been accepted by local sportsman and hunters who are shooting hundreds every favorable day.

"Impressed by the unusual opportunity to wipe out thousands of enemies to bird and game life in the State, a Pottsville sportsman today urged local hunters to cooperate in killing hawks.

"The migrating birds pass within a few feet of the ground at the mountain pinnacle, generally between the hours of 10 A.M. and 3 P.M., only when a stiff northwest wind is blowing.

With ordinary shotguns, 300 hawks were killed last Friday . . .

"For years, hunters have been seeking the spot in the Blue Mountains over which the hawks pass in their migration to the south. Finally discovering the place, a number have almost daily congregated and poured many boxes of shells into the blackened skies, killing as many as eight with a single bullet. . . ."

The "sportsman" was reputed also to be a sporting goods merchant, doing a lucrative business selling shells to the local sportsmen who accepted the challenge of the hawks which were brashly "inviting extermination." It is interesting to note the familiarity with basic details of the hawk flights, such as requisite wind conditions and the best time of day to be on hand. The slaughter is condoned with the usual falsehood concerning "enemies to bird and game life."

A news item similar to this, reprinted in a Philadelphia newspaper, attracted two young conservationists of that city, Henry H. Collins, Jr., and Richard H. Pough. During the fall of 1932 they made five trips to the Blue Mountain, above Drehersville. These were no pleasure jaunts such as people make nowadays. Collins and Pough were amazed and shocked. They were mad enough, too, to give prompt, vigorous expression to their investigations. Collins, in the *Bulletin of the Hawk and Owl Society* for 1933, called the attention of conversationists to the wanton slaughter.

"The season extends from early September to December," Collins wrote. "The height appears to be during the first weeks of October. On one occasion, sixty-four automobiles, the means of transportation of over two hundred gunners, were parked along the mountain road. On another occasion there were forty cars, with about one hundred and fifty hunters, including twelve women.

"The hunting has been going on for many years. It appears to have grown in popularity since the World War, but one hunter spoke of his father shooting there as far back as sixty years ago.

"One case of extreme cruelty witnessed was that of a wounded hawk tied to a log. When another hawk appeared in the sky, a man would jab the wounded bird with a stick to make it scream and thus attract its fellow migrant to a similar fate. Such cruelty is illegal under the humane laws of the State and all engaged in it are liable as accomplices. Wardens on duty, however, have never made any attempt to stop it. Another decoy consisted of a hawk thrown into a tree by means of a stone on a string and left dangling there in the northwest breeze.

"Wardens, if on duty, will call out, 'It's an osprey. Don't shoot!' but usually a gun goes off anyway. The bird is killed, and in the confusion among so many hunters the guilty one usually escapes."

Blinded pigeons were also commonly used to decoy the hawks at the various shooting-stands. The pigeons were tied to a long pole, and when an approaching hawk was sighted the hunter waved the pole, causing the pigeon to flutter wildly. Almost any bird of prey could readily be lured into the gun sights by such means. Such practices are still commonly employed elsewhere in the mountains of Pennsylvania where hawk-shooting persists.

While Pough and Collins were making their investigations, the S. P. C. A. was urged to stop the hawk-shooting. This organization arranged with the State Police to have two members of the police force on duty atop the mountain. If the policemen expected to halt the horror, they might as well have tried to stop the flow of black waters of the little river winding along the foot of the mountain. Years later I was to meet one of these gentlemen, Ernest Barr of Philadelphia. He told me, "We spent three nightmarish weeks on this mountain. There were as many as four hundred hunters one day, and so many birds were slaughtered that a bad odor hung over the place. We couldn't do a thing about it." So the holocaust continued.

On Sundays, if the flight was good, few birds succeeded in running the gauntlet of the bloodthirsty mob. Earl L. Poole, Director of the Reading Museum, who became familiar with the locality in the early '30's, reported: "On such days (Sundays) the roar of the guns is almost continuous and resembles a Fourth-of-July celebration on a vast scale. The consensus of opinion among those who have taken part in these 'hawk-shoots' over a number of years is that only a quarter as many fly past this point now as could be seen eight years ago. Little wonder! The lamentable feature of this slaughter is that most of the victims are not even picked up as they fall, but allowed to decompose or serve as food for foxes, skunks, opossums, cave-rats, mice and shrews that live in the rocks. Many of them are merely wounded and allowed to die a lingering and miserable death. . . . During September hundreds of the distinctly beneficial broad-wings are butchered in the same manner, and in October many ospreys, red-tailed and red-shouldered hawks and eagles receive the same treatment."

Each fall a local resident would drive a truckload of cartridges up the mountain and ply a brisk trade. Other men, equally anxious to profit, gathered up the used shells to salvage the old brass.

Blind men! Unfolding before their eyes was the mystery, the eternal wonder of migration. But they could not see. What meant it to them, the bold, impetuous speed of the peregrine? Of what account the grace and fluency of osprey moving down the sky? Or the wings of an eagle slanting into the west like the sails of a galleon? Leonardo da Vinci perceived aerodynamics in the vibrant vans of the *Buteo;* but to these men—nonsense, *kill it!* The sky-borne freedom of the falcon was to be stopped and shattered by a shower of lead. The fierce purity of the wilderness reduced to mangled feathers on blood-stained rocks. . . .

This was sport. This was an opportunity to exhibit skill in marksmanship, to train the eye of the gunner for the coming game-killing season. Besides, so-called "sportsmen" and certain farmers considered it their divine right to kill every hawk. Were not all hawks "vermin," a plague to small game which God created especially for the hunters?

The hawks were not destroying property and were not even residents in Pennsylvania. The hunters were killing birds that belonged to the nation, and more specifically to the inhabitants of regions to the north and south, where the hawks summer and winter. But these hunters had no scruples; they merely expressed an atavistic urge to destroy. Untold thousands of the birds had been massacred on this mountain peak during the sixty to seventy years of its desecration—and only three voices had been raised to save them.

Here was a dramatic opportunity to put an end to the horror. Who would make conservation history? A full year passed. In October, 1933, at a joint meeting of the Hawk and Owl Society, the National Association of Audubon Societies and the Linnaen Society of New York, Richard Pough, anxious to save the birds, reported that he had made contact with real estate agents of the owners of the mountain. The property could be bought at a low figure and on easy terms. Conservationists present at this meeting were confident that the problem was solved. But nothing happened to quiet the roar of guns above Drehersville.

The spring and early summer of 1934 passed, and still nothing was done. But one woman's sleep had been tormented with visions of the birds gasping in agony or blown to bits in the skies.

Mrs. Charles Noel Edge, of New York City, now moved in on the field of battle. Mrs. Edge was, and still is, chairman of the militant Emergency Conservation Committee which had performed prodigies for wildlife protection. In a span of only five years the Committee had campaigned to save our vanishing waterfowl; had fought for the preservation of elk in our national parks; the saving of Yosemite sugar pines; had worked to save the bald eagle; had sent the antelope's S. O. S. across the country; and had made a plea for effective guardianship and preservation of certain of our national parks. Mrs. Edge, as the Committee's chairman, was indefatigable.

In August of that year, Mrs. Edge obtained, without difficulty, a lease of the mountain for one year, with an option to buy from the owners, two elderly brothers in Habelton, Pennsylvania. The property acquired, the next problem was the pressing one of getting someone before mid-September to protect it.

Mrs. Broun and I had been spending a pleasant summer in Vermont. Our holiday was electrified in mid-August by an urgent letter from Mrs. Edge, asking me if I would assume wardenship that autumn. "We must have a warden on the property: first to post it and then to guard it and get police protection. It is a job that needs some courage," she wrote to me.

An exciting prospect, but a hazardous one. We decided on hopping from the Green Mountains to the Blue Mountains. I replied that we would "take over" without salary; the Emergency Conservation Committee could pay our expenses, I suggested. Mrs. Edge, on the eve of her departure on a trip to Panama, wrote to us enthusiastically of her satisfaction that we would tackle the situation at "Hawk Mountain," but she warned, "I anticipate you will have real trouble with lawless hunters and I recommend that you get promptly in touch with the Pennsylvania State Police and ask for protection on Saturdays and Sundays." On her way to the steamer, Mrs. Edge stopped at her lawyers and signed a power of attorney giving me authority and a free hand at Hawk Mountain during her absence.

Thus "Hawk Mountain" Sanctuary came into being—the world's first sanctuary for the birds of prey. It marks an epoch in conservation.

2

ARRIVAL AT
HAWK MOUNTAIN

A gentle, sunny forenoon in early September found us in the vicinity of Drehersville, about to begin a series of adventures. Our journey had taken us through the dreary coal regions. Now our spirits quickened and our eyes opened with wonder as we approached our destination. Here were lush farmlands, the renowned red hills of Pennsylvania, glowing in the morning sun. We slowed down to admire the barns, decorated with large circles, enclosing multi-lobed stars. These are the hex symbols of the Pennsylvania Dutch. They are supposed to ward off evil spirits and lightning, but one kindly farmer told us that they are "just for nice." Driving along, we had occasional glimpses of the women, wearing quaint sunbonnets and gracious smiles. Any fears that we might have entertained about the formidable task at "Hawk Mountain" were quieted by the charm and beauty of the countryside.

At a farmhouse within a mile of Drehersville, we asked a bonneted *Frau* the way to "Hawk Mountain." Bewilderment spread over her broad countenance as she weighed the question, and perhaps the strange manner of speech of outlanders. "Ach, I dunno. Dere iss the Blue Mountain," she said, pointing a stubby finger toward a wooded ridge-top extending in a long, dark line above and just beyond one of the rich red hills that dipped into her very dooryard.

Drehersville, a cluster of tidy houses surrounding a tiny church, lay dozing under the hot September sun. Hardly a soul was in sight. Hushed tranquillity, deep repose, the feeling that all was well with the world pervaded the little village. This was not at all what we had anticipated; this was alien to what we had read about: blood and thunder, and swarms of gun-toting men.

The sudden banging and rattling of a long train of coal cars on the narrow railroad, back of the church, released us from our musings. Beyond the railroad and the winding, sulphurous Little Schuylkill River, which spills out of the near-by coal regions laden with culm, loomed a dark spur of the mountain. This, we surmised, must be the end of our trail; we headed the car over a bridge and up over a rough mountain road with sharp turns and steep grades.

In those days, and for several years thereafter, the road over the mountain was extremely narrow, full of "thank-you-ma'ams" and sharp, angular rocks that tore savagely at one's tires. I shall never forget our first ascent of that terrible, seemingly endless road, the forest crowding in on both sides. Two deer bounded ahead of us and vanished. No houses or sign of any human beings.

As the car labored up the mountain, we wondered anew whether this could really be the place that attracted so many hawks and so many hawk-hunters. At length we reached the summit and got out to survey the wild and lonely prospect. Yes, this must be the place, for shotgun shells were scattered everywhere. But the old Turner house, which Mrs. Edge had mentioned in one of her letters as a likely place to find accommodations—where was it? It seemed incredible that anyone might live up here.

The road made a sudden dip toward the east, and in a few minutes we came abruptly upon an old stone house, alongside the road, in a dimple of the mountain.

Unlike the neat, trim houses of the valley, this isolated dwelling had about it an air of gloom and disintegration. Anxiously, my wife and I, and our dog Cubby, got out of the car. The sour smell of dishwater thrown into the dusty road indicated the lack of plumbing. Flies hummed all over the place. But there was no time to stare or to wonder; there was a job to be done.

The place was tenanted by a pleasant, middle-aged woman, her two beaming grandchildren and their father, a man in his mid-twenties.

"Where's the place where the hawks are killed?" I asked. The woman waved a hand toward a pinnacle, clearly visible a full mile north of the house.

"Is this the Turner place?"

"It used to be," she replied in a tired voice.

We did not tell her why we had come, but timidly, almost hesitantly, we asked whether we might find temporary lodging with her. "Temporary" until we could get oriented in this novel situation. Mrs. Merkle, for that was her name, said she could accommodate us. She showed us into the house, explaining that it belonged to a man named Wenz, who lived in Allentown. She took care of the house. It was drab and dim and cluttered. We climbed a narrow stairway to the attic, which was dark and as hot as the inside of an oven. This was where we could sleep. My wife Irma and I exchanged apprehensive glances. Well, for a few nights. . . .

We were famished after our long, hard morning trying to locate the mountain. Mrs. Merkle was low on foodstuffs, but soon had her kitchen table spread for lunch, which consisted of some wan turnips, bread and elderberry jam, and milk. I stole another glance at my wife, and her wide eyes searched mine as if to ask, "What are we in for?"

Mrs. Merkle proved to be the soul of friendliness; but we felt that her cooking was hopeless and that her housekeeping was, perhaps, worse. The old house seemed cluttered, moreover, with an assortment of unrelated furnishings that had long since seen better days. The grounds were littered with debris suggesting numerous clambakes and drinking parties. We tried to look cheerful, but the whole place, and the uncertainties of the weeks ahead, induced only depression. Had anyone suggested that some day we would call this "home," and like it, too, I am sure that my wife would have dropped flat on her face!

Luncheon over, we had the entire afternoon ahead of us, and it seemed urgent to me that we make the most of it. I decided that we had better run into Schuylkill Haven, some twelve miles toward Pottsville, to call on the real estate agent. We had hoped to learn from him about the mountain. We also needed quantities of "no-trespassing" posters.

My first act in Schuylkill Haven was to phone four local newspapers, requesting each to carry a notice, for three successive days, announcing the new status of the mountain property, that it was henceforth an inviolate wildlife sanctuary, and that the trespass laws would be enforced. Then we called on Gordon Reed, the agent for the property. Oh, yes, he knew all about the mountain and all about the hawk-shoots; and he succeeded in filling us with gloom. I told him that I was about to put up no-trespassing posters along the road, especially at the beginning of the trail that led through the woods to the shooting stands. When we parted, Mr. Reed suggested, "After you get your posters up, take my advice and *scram!*"

That evening, after a vague meal, we sat dejectedly in Mrs. Merkle's kitchen. The oil lamp made only a pretense of throwing light into the shadowy corners. Mrs. Merkle and her son sat playing cards. The children had been put to bed in the attic. Soon Irma and I, completely fagged from a day of questing, took to our bed in a separate chamber of the attic. And what an attic! A battered tin roof crowded down upon us, blistering hot from the late summer sun's beating upon it all day. For ventilation there was a single tiny window, and a multitude of nail-holes in the roof. The torrid night air was swollen with the odor from the outdoor privy, just a few feet below the window. The confused chorus of katydids delayed our sleep.

That night the elements unbuckled. Lightning flicked through the little window, lighting up the shabby plaster walls. Rain in torrents beat a lively tattoo on the tin roof. Rain trickled through the nail-holes onto our wobbly bed. It was a miserable situation for a bride of but a few months. But, as Irma remarked ruefully in the small hours of the morning, it could have been worse. She was always a good sport.

Early morning found me putting up posters along the rocky road. Where did the bounds of the property run through the woods? Not even the neighboring owners could tell exactly. Five years later a costly survey revealed to us the extent of the 1398 acres. For the time being, it was necessary to post both sides of a stretch of road one and a half miles; for the road, a public thoroughfare, bisected the Sanctuary. It was dreadfully hot. I was surprised that no hunters had come. I did not know that it was too early in the season, nor did I realize that the hawk-hunters knew just when to flock to the mountain.

By mid-afternoon the lonely road flaunted posters every few yards. A local game warden, apparently startled by my newspaper notices which had just been printed, came to find out what it was all about. The warden tried to impress me with the utter futility of my job. "Wait till the coal-miners from Tamaqua come along; then you'll see," he warned me. While we argued, two carloads of hunters drove up—the vanguard. I explained that hunting of all kinds was henceforth prohibited. There was much guttural, explosive language from the visitors. But they left the mountain, bewildered, to say the least. In the days to follow I was to meet many such men, many of whom I tried to reason with as to why hawks should not be killed indiscriminately. Generally, these men were irritated, unwilling to listen. The game warden, a man named Jones, concluded his visit with the statement that I had the hardest job on my hands that I'd ever have in my life. "You can't stop those guys from shooting hawks up here," he said, notwithstanding that I had already done so, before his eyes!

It suddenly came to me that, after all, in spite of our right, our duty to stop the hawk-shooting, we were, from the standpoint of the hunters, meddlesome outsiders, and as such we were bound to arouse indignation. Of course, it did not matter to the hunters that most of the hawks also came down from New England and New York. Did they ever give a thought to the rights of others?

Before the close of the day I prepared a thousand-word statement—"A New Deal for Hawks"—defending the action of the Emergency Conservation Committee in leasing the mountaintop to prevent the killing of hawks. It hammered out the theme of unjust persecution and the economic importance of the hawks. Every trip up and down the mountain was agony and torture to tires, but I sent the article off the same evening to three local newspapers, whose combined circulation exceeded 200,000. The article promptly appeared in print, and it was copied in other newspapers, as far away as Scranton.

Daybreak of our third day on the mountain found me patrolling the road! I was anxious to see some hawks, but I was utterly ignorant of the hawk-flights and their *modus operandi.* And, naïvely, I expected to see hunters at that ridiculous hour. During the night someone had ripped off most of the no-trespassing posters.

At breakfast, a few staccato shots echoed from the pinnacle that Mrs. Merkle had pointed out to us. I dashed up the road and through the woods, over an exceedingly rough but well-trodden path to the pinnacle. There I found a young man and his father, from Allentown, settled behind a huge rock slab. Their presence was pardonable, since the posters had been abstracted. And were they surprised to learn that the area was now a sanctuary! Had they killed any hawks? Not yet—the birds had just begun to come. They departed like gentlemen after—of all things—a brief discussion of the geology of the region, about which I confessed that I knew less than they. Then for the first time I saw the great rock promontory, and the scene that suddenly spread out before me was one of great beauty. The early morning haze partly curtained the ridge, but a thousand feet below me I saw numbers of white leghorns ranging the neat, pastel patchworks of farmland. If the hawks were so destructive, as claimed by the game warden and the hunters, what in the name of chicken à la king were all those fowl doing where "chicken hawks" were as prevalent as sparrows in a barnyard?

As I patrolled the road that day, replacing posters, I was impressed with the countless numbers of old cartridge shells scattered along a quarter-mile stretch of road above the present entrance to the Sanctuary. In the early afternoon I was thrilled to see my first flight of hawks, some fifty birds, including three bald eagles, three peregrine falcons, a few broad-wings and sharp-shins, all passing fairly low over the road. This *was* exciting!

During the day three more cars came up, with seven inquiring faces, and shotguns ready for business. But they departed promptly. One of the men made a slurring remark about the "New York chiselers going to hog all the shooting."

My wife spent the afternoon with me, near the summit of the road. We had enjoyed the sight of more hawks in a few hours than we could see ordinarily in an entire year. We marveled at the winged hosts sailing over.

Evening came on quickly. Again we sat in Mrs. Merkle's gloomy kitchen. By now our hostess knew our purpose in coming to "Hawk Mountain." I believe that she thought we were "teched in the head" to want to risk life and limb to save hawks. But she was exceedingly good-natured and, what was better, she was neutral about the "nervy foreigners" who expected to keep hunters off the mountain. So we sat, in pleasant conversation.

Mrs. Merkle had had many interesting experiences during several summers and falls spent on the mountain. She used to sit on the back porch with a shotgun and pop off rats and rattlesnakes. There was one rattlesnake not so ill-fated, however. She told us a tale that made our spines tingle. One day she went to the doorway to call one of her grandchildren, who had been playing in the road. There was the child, sitting in the road, a snake in her lap. A rattlesnake! With rare presence of mind, Mrs. Merkle said or did nothing to distract the child or the snake. She simply watched, fascinated, with breathless anxiety, until the snake, tiring of being fondled by the child, slithered off.

A rap on the door, which opened in from the dark road, interrupted us. Mrs. Merkle admitted three burly figures smelling of whiskey and carrying shotguns which they leaned ostentatiously against the walls. They talked to her in Pennsylvania Dutch. Though we could not understand a word, we realized that the conversation concerned the two "foreigners." Just before they left, they turned to me and one of them switching to English, suggested, "This ain't a healthy place. You'd better leave the mountain soon or we might have to shoot you off!"

Whatever the three musketeers had put across to Mrs. Merkle we never did know, but she was in a pretty bad state of nerves the next morning. At breakfast she said that she could no longer keep us; and then she broke down in tears. She said we'd better leave right away; perhaps we might find a place to stay in Drehersville. Three nights in that attic were enough for us, so we lost no time in getting packed, settled up with our friend, said good-bye and headed the car for the village. As we tumbled down the nearly impossible road, our spirits tumbled, too; we felt that everyone would turn us away—we, the absurd, unwelcome protectors of hawks!

Our first stop in Drehersville was at the little general store and post office, next to the church. The elderly store-owner, Mr. Marberger, had already heard about the queer people from Massachusetts who had come to stop the hawk-shooting. We were heartened by the old man's open friendliness. When we told him that we had spent three nights at the old house on the mountain, he asked "Weren't you afraid?" (We were plenty afraid, but for reasons other than he was thinking).

"Why, what was there to be afraid of?" I asked.

"Oh, that old place is haunted," he explained. "They say that years ago a German named Schaumboch killed eleven people up there. Everyone around here knows the place is haunted." He was amazed that we had survived three nights in the old house. And so were we! In later years we were to hear all kinds of weird tales about "Schaumboch's"—for henceforth that was to be the name we heard most frequently in connection with the ancient cottage.

"Can you tell us where we can find room and board near

by?" I asked the old man. After a moment's reflection he pointed out a large white house within walking distance.

So we walked up to a neat and freshly-painted dwelling, as solid-looking as some of the natives. Yet, it had a certain uninviting aspect, with all its windows closed and the blinds drawn. I knocked on the door. No answer. I knocked again, remembering that the storekeeper assured us that someone would be home. And still no answer.

As we stood there, a young woman of dour countenance walked up to the doorway, deposited two bottles of milk and whisked about without acknowledging our "Good morning!" Could she tell us whether anyone might be at home? No answer, and she passed briskly down a cement walk. I caught up with her, but further attempts to extract information from this sphinx-like person were as hopeful as pulling trout out of the culm-choked Schuylkill. In silence she came, in silence she withdrew, without so much as a friendly glance at us. So we returned to the store.

"Nobody home," I told Mr. Marberger. "But we met the queerest woman who wouldn't speak or even look at us," chimed in my wife.

"Oh, that was my daughter; she's deaf!" explained the storekeeper, with complete indifference. Receiving further instructions from the kindly old fellow to visit the home of the Kochs, about a half mile distant, we took off quickly, embarrassment written all over us.

As we rolled along the country roads, made muddy by a series of hard rains, our eyes lighted up as we approached a massive stone house surrounded by attractively arranged flower-beds, across the road from an immense red barn. A perfect rural picture, we thought, and how inviting—except for the seven cats we counted as we drove into the yard. Irma said, "They won't take us here when they see Cubby." Cubby was our chow-sized, extremely energetic, mischievous mongrel. The thought of being turned away filled me with visions of pitching a tent somewhere on the mountain.

The Kochs were sitting at their kitchen table, busily making chowchow, a favorite Pennsylvania Dutch relish. A large kettle of it was boiling on the stove and filling the house with a wonderful, spicy aroma. Walter Koch's massive paunch was something to wonder at, as it almost rested on the table; there was impish humor and kindliness in his blue eyes. Mrs. Koch, a sturdy, dimpled little woman, wore a blue sunbonnet, a blue apron, and a look of genuine good will.

"Maybe you've heard about us; we're the hawk people. We've stayed at the little house on the mountain but we are looking for a place to stay down here. I might as well tell you, though," I added with deep misgivings, "that we've come to stop the hawk-shooting on the mountain."

"Ach yes, ve heard about youse," said Mrs. Koch, with a broad grin that dispelled all our fears. "Ve'll take you."

"Oh, but we have a dog—is that all right?" asked Irma uneasily, as she surveyed the numerous cats.

"Ach, vell, ve haff ten cats, but they von't hurt nothing. You can come in once," was Mrs. Koch's ready settlement of the cat-and-dog question. We took to the Kochs immediately, won by their simplicity and friendliness, and I think they took to us. To our surprise, Farmer Koch told us that he had always disapproved of the hawk-shoots. Two of his sons used to go up to the mountain to kill hawks, he said, and it always irked him because he considered it a waste of time and money.

The comfortable Koch home was an invitation to relaxation; to cross its threshold was to enter the quaint, delightful realm of the Pennsylvania Dutch.

3 # THE
BARBARIANS

It was a blessing to be comfortably settled with the Kochs. At last we could relax; it had been utterly impossible to do so on the mountain, at "Schaumboch's." And Mrs. Koch's food! Her large square table groaned under the weight of a variety of foods, which included several kinds of meat, chicken, eggs, relishes, jams, pies, cake and cookies; and we came to know those traditional Pennsylvania Dutch achievements: shoo-fly pie, apple butter and scrapple. Irma said it was like a visit to a foreign country. Mrs. Koch beamed and told us not once, but many times, how "proud" she was that we enjoyed her food. To be "proud" was to be pleased.

Walter Koch was not so "proud," however. He had just returned from Marberger's store where, late in the day, many of the neighbors foregathered for cracker-barrel chatter of current events. The *fahricht* (crazy) couple from Massachusetts had become a sensational current event, and the air in Drehersville was charged with the hottest kind of argument. The menfolk did not approve of the Kochs providing us with board and shelter. So the Kochs found themselves the center of a stormy discussion, all because of the "foreigners." But Walter Koch, a man of courage and independent mind, was our stanch ally; at the risk of becoming most unpopular with his neighbors, he defended our position. He warned us that we were in for a lot of trouble; possibly the coming week end.

The following morning I found that every single one of my sixty-odd posters along the road had been removed. It began to rain, for which I rejoiced, since no one was likely to venture up the mountain to make trouble. I drove into Hamburg, the nearest large town, to obtain more posters, and to make contact with game wardens and the State Police. I thought, naïvely, that I could obtain official protection on week ends.

"You can't keep gunners off that land, and I wouldn't take your job for a hundred dollars a day!" exclaimed Game Protector Dressner as I interviewed him in his home. I explained that I was doing the job for nothing—"just expenses." Dressner was dumbfounded. After a minute of silence, he phoned another game warden, who came promptly. The situation was so novel and amusing to both wardens— outsiders protecting hawks, and in control of a whole mountaintop to do so—that they guffawed. They were as sympathetic as crows that had discovered an owl. Since they, too, joined in the hawk-shoots, it was useless to appeal to them for help. Then how about the State Police? I went over to the police barracks and learned that the police had their hands full with strikes in the local industries. Dressner had assured me that the police had been known to participate in the hawk-shooting.

(I did not see Dressner again for thirteen years. Then, on a Sunday in November, he and his family appeared at the Sanctuary summit rocks. I recognized him instantly, which so surprised Dressner that he was again dumbfounded. When he recovered from his surprise, we reminisced pleasantly. Dressner had long since given up shooting hawks, and game protection, too, for fruit-growing. He confided to me that on that first meeting he was sure we were crackpots, certain to have a brief and violent career on that mountain.)

The rain came down steadily, a comfort. I returned to the Koch farm, to rest in our large, inviting room. But I could not rest. I was worried and I had a queasy, inadequate feeling, which did not, however, derive from lack of experience. I had had abundant experience with trespassers and game-law violators, at various wildlife refuges in New England. But this situation was far more complex; it involved the interests of hundreds, possibly thousands, of organized, politically-ruled men who were certain to boil up in anger and resentment at the intrusion of a small, to them un-heard-of, organization which had suddenly seized "their" entire mountain. Though we possessed maps and land titles, the location of the twelve miles of boundaries of the wilderness property was anybody's guess. Were we sitting on a powder keg? To withdraw was unthinkable. Glumly I pondered the whole picture, and the words of Shakespeare: "Wrens make prey where eagles dare not perch."

The week end was upon us. I drove up the mountain after breakfast and in a drizzling rain I managed to nail up an entirely new set of posters. The weather cleared in the early afternoon. A few hawks passed low over the road. Only two cars appeared, each emptying gunners—five in one car. These men asked if they could walk to the pinnacle, and I allowed them to do so, without their guns. Returning, an old man in the group had this to offer: "A fellow doesn't want a gun up there; he should bring a pair of field glasses and a camera." These were the first heartening words I had heard on the mountain since our arrival.

Sunday brought raw, nasty weather, which suited me immensely. At 5 A.M. I was at my post of duty on the mountain road, expecting hunters and the promised trouble. It began to rain again, so I returned to the Kochs' for breakfast. And back up the mountain after breakfast. In those days I was cursed with a New England conscience. Nothing happened, except the weather, and obligingly it poured all through the day. While I guarded the road, Irma attended the local (Lutheran) church with the Kochs. Some seventy natives were in attendance, and how they stared at my wife. From then on she was known as the "hawk-woman."

Looking back on those early, disquieting experiences, I marvel at our great good luck with the weather. Providentially, torrents of rain fell on three successive week ends, and the anticipated hordes of hawk-killers did not materialize. The game wardens had warned me, however, that early October would bring plenty of hawks and plenty of trouble in the form of toughs from the coal region.

Mrs. Edge and her son Peter came out to the mountain in the middle of the second week to see how everything had been going. The situation was well in hand, and we had had no trouble—not yet—but it behooved us to engage a deputy sheriff, I advised Mrs. Edge. Obviously we must secure the services of someone who was authorized to make arrests, if necessary. I had already begun to cast around for the right man and, through the help of a sympathetic notary in a near-by town, I hoped to engage Bob Kramer, if Mrs. Edge approved. And she did. The cost of maintaining Kramer for ten weeks was another worry for Mrs. Edge, but she did not hesitate.

Bob Kramer, of near-by Auburn, a sturdy man of forty-two, good-humored and dependable, possessed an important weapon which I lacked: the Pennsylvania Dutch tongue. He had been engaged in police work for years. Kramer would have agreed to work for us on week ends only, but we took him on daily, beginning the end of September. I also engaged a surveyor, who successfully determined our im-

portant west boundary, the one nearest the hunters of Drehersville.

Meanwhile I continued my vigil, day after day, at the entrance to the Sanctuary, where few hawks are seen unless the
wind is in a southerly quarter. All sorts of men with high-
powered rifles and shotguns came to indulge in the old
"sport," only to learn that on *this* mountain it was a thing of
the past. A few hunters came from New Jersey, and two
from Delaware. My tongue wagged incessantly those first
few weeks. It was no fun trying to convince those men of
the folly of shooting hawks. Many were surly, and some went
off with pent-up truculence. My only weapons that entire
season were a ready tongue and a bold front—under which I
sometimes quailed! But Kramer had a gun which was
respected.

The evening of the seventeenth two young men dropped
in at the Kochs' and said they had been gunning a few miles
up the ridge, during the afternoon. They asked me whether
I had seen the big hawk flight. No, I had not. Then I
learned that they had counted almost two thousand hawks
passing high over the ridge that afternoon; a broad-wing
flight, I gathered. I was chagrined that I had missed the
spectacle. Not until October 7th did I make daily visits to
the mountain summit to observe the wonderful hawk-flights,
while Kramer patrolled the road.

The possibility of an "invasion" of hunters now became
very real. Kramer's daily presence had deterred the local
hotheads from forcing their way; but Walter Koch, who always knew what was going on and warned us accordingly,
advised me that it might be necessary for me to stand guard
at the old shooting-stands on the crest of the mountain.
From there it was possible to observe the various approaches
to the summit, through the woods from the north or from
the west.

One day I learned from Mr. Koch, almost with disbelief, that a certain obstreperous character in Drehersville, who worked cheek by jowl with the officials of the numerous hunting clubs, had been obtaining sworn affidavits from many of the local farmers that the hawks often came down and carried off young pigs! This same man killed a red-tailed hawk and, to taunt us, he hung the bird, with wings spread, from the girders of the little bridge over which we passed twice daily. There the bird hung for about ten days. I took a picture of it which helped us in our money-raising campaign.

Now a great hullabaloo was raised in gunning circles throughout two counties against the out-of-state "chiselers." The farmers in the vicinity made the loudest squawk. They not only resented us and our assumed arrogance in taking over "their" mountain, they resented the name "Hawk Mountain" and claimed that there never had been such a place. Local newspapers belabored us and carried the usual stale message that the hawks were killing off the game. A great to-do was made by the Pottsville merchant "sportsman" who used to come up the mountain on week ends, his truck loaded with cartridges to sell. We learned that the local sportsmen's clubs, representing 15,000 hunters, had engaged a lawyer to search all land titles and find loopholes which might break Mrs. Edge's lease, and to buy the mountain, if possible. The hunters were holding frequent meetings to decide what to do.

A few days later, the agitated hawk-shooters, though still contemplating the purchase of "Hawk Mountain," leased a considerable tract of land near Port Clinton. I saw their advertisement in a newspaper, urging gunners to kill hawks in this new place, about four miles down the ridge, and offering gunners "a new line of shells, at .60 a case." Kramer investigated the Port Clinton hawk-shoots. These could be serious on days when the wind was easterly, but at no time was the slaughter comparable to that which had occurred formerly on our mountain. The place was also much more difficult of access.

Most of the hunters that I encountered had been killing hawks on this mountain for many years. Most of them were obdurate in their opinion of hawks in general and, they insisted, all hawks should be exterminated. It was useless to argue that the hawks do not feed while migrating, and that the food habits of the birds of prey involved mainly rodents. One farmer, in spite of his carping, allowed his large flock of white leghorns to roam the fields at the foot of the mountain. Why, I asked the gunners, were there so many grouse drumming in these upland woods? Here, at the greatest concentration point for hawks in the entire country, the ruffed grouse abounded; one day I had counted thirty-three of the birds in different parts of the Sanctuary. Rabbits, quail and pheasants were plentiful in the excellent cover of the old fields in the vicinity of Drehersville. But perhaps I was "seeing things," for the hawks kill off the game!

In early October much of the opposition had quieted, but it looked like the calm before the storm, and throughout the month Kramer and I anticipated trouble daily. Mr. Koch shook his head apprehensively. (I think that during that whole season Walter Koch did more worrying about the "hawk people" than we did about ourselves.) The fourth week end was approaching, and Mr. Koch was sure that this week end we would have trouble. A group of local hunters was planning to mob Kramer and me and force their way to the summit.

Late Friday afternoon two husky young men, built like fullbacks, appeared without guns at the Sanctuary. I was pleasantly surprised to learn that they had been recruited by Richard Pough to help us protect the place for a week or so.

Pough, one of the "discoverers" of the hawk-shoots, had been in constant touch with Mrs. Edge. Knowing only too well what we might be up against with the lawless elements among the hawk-shooters, Pough generously arranged to have Charlie French and Dudley Wagar, both of Philadelphia, help us. Mrs. Koch cheerfully provided accommodations for the two young men.

The following day it poured again—the fourth soggy Saturday! The four of us, Kramer, the newcomers and I spent a few hours on the mountain road, nevertheless, hunched in our cars. We even turned away a few hunters who had come from Reading. Back at the farmhouse I asked Mr. Koch if he thought the weather would clear. "Maurice, it always has," said he with a chuckle. In the evening he returned from Marberger's store with a twinkle in his eyes and a knowing grin. It was being bruited around the village that we had engaged two detectives.

Sunday, October 7th, brought beautiful weather and ideal hawking conditions. Kramer and Wagar took the road, while French and I posted ourselves at the summit rocks. It was a day of many surprises, and some drama—but not the drama we had expected. We had plenty of company, some of it very talented. Ten members of the Delaware Valley Ornithological Club, of Philadelphia, including Richard Pough, Samuel Scoville, Jr., the writer, Julian K. Potter, the ornithologist, and Jacob B. Abbott, the artist, were among the observers at the Lookout that day. The hawk flight was disappointing—only a hundred birds of thirteen species. But to me it was tremendously exciting to see so many kinds of hawks. A special feature was an adult golden eagle. The great bird came obligingly close, an eye-opener to the ornithological gathering—and the first of many golden eagles that were to lure bird watchers from all over the country.

Early in the afternoon we heard some shooting on the

ridge-top, about a half mile directly behind us. Charlie French and I and one of the D. V. O. C. men took off through the woods and presently we reached the west boundary of the Sanctuary. There, on the edge of our line, marked by no-trespassing posters, were ten men, two of them perched high in a tree, blazing away at occasional hawks passing just out of shotgun range. The men were just off the Sanctuary property. There was nothing I could do, except perhaps to wait until they might kill a protected species (ten ospreys and a bald eagle were the only "protected" birds that passed), and then I would prosecute the killer. So we leaned against a tree and waited, silently. The shooting stopped, the men were maddened that we just stood there and stared at them. Each passing minute increased the tension till one of the men snapped, "Well, whatcha goin' to do about it?" I replied, "Just stay here and see what you fellows might do." The fellow lowered his gun, came up to me menacingly and said, "I'll knock your —— block off." For a moment it looked like a fight—and it might have been bad business, three unarmed men against ten with guns and hot tempers—but the fellow suddenly stopped and spluttered, "You damn hawk-lovers; you're just a bunch of barbarians." How we three unarmed men laughed! I warned the men not to be caught trespassing, and I withdrew with my companions.

Returning to the Lookout, I found more visitors. A "mob" had indeed come! That day seventy-four men, women and children climbed to the Lookout to enjoy the beautiful scenery and the birds. It was an inspiring sight, and it augured well for the successful outcome of our "new deal for the hawks." At the entrance, Kramer had turned away thirty-two gunners, including a few women. Ten times that number of gunners, might have been on hand that day had we not spent the previous weeks impressing the hunting elements that we meant business on the mountain. Pleasant week ends thereafter brought increasing numbers of bird-students and protectionists to enjoy the hawking.

Hawk-hunters, some of them hard-bitten fellows who looked as though they would as soon shoot a mother-in-law as a hawk, continued to come late into November—a month *after* the opening of the small game season—so deep-rooted was the urge to follow this perverse and cruel "sport." But in spite of all the threats and warnings and the hubbub of the shotgun squads, we had a singularly peaceful time of it along the old mountain road. At the summit, in the few weeks that it was possible to observe the hawk-flights, we had the satisfaction of seeing more than ten thousand hawks pass safely; not a single bird was killed. Not a single untoward incident occurred in that birth-year of the Sanctuary.

Mrs. Edge's coup in obtaining the mountain and our efforts in safeguarding it were an undreamed-of success. Kramer's help was a godsend, my wife's patience and courage were an inspiration, the Kochs were a blessing (especially invaluable was Walter Koch's tapping of the grapevine), and Mrs. Edge's financial and moral support insured victory. In the end, Mrs. Edge remunerated us generously, though we had not expected a cent beyond our expenses. The National Audubon Society, the Massachusetts Audubon Society, the New Jersey Audubon Society, the Linnaean Society of New York, and many individuals, of whom the most openhanded was Dr. Willard G. Van Name, came to Mrs. Edge's aid with needed funds. So ended in triumph our initial adventures in conservation at Hawk Mountain Sanctuary.

THE KEEPER
CHAPTER 4 OF THE GATE

She accompanied me on bird banding trips. She was slight and wiry and as quick as a bird; and she was unbanded. Day after day, in the hot July sun, we combed the Cape Cod beaches, banding tern chicks, hundreds of them, and often we trapped adult terns on their nests. The terns protested, screamed, and dive-bombed at our heads, sometimes drawing blood with their stiletto-like beaks. But the slight little lady never protested.

Then followed visits to night heron rookeries—pestilential places of grunts and groans and juvenal screams and gagging. Entering a rookery to band fledgling herons usually meant penetrating tangles of thorny smilax and poison ivy, creeping with wood ticks. Perilous climbing among nests from which squirted globs of whitewash! Fetid fumes from decaying fish. And swarms of mosquitoes and deer-flies to complete the torture. The fringe of lunacy, and no place for a lady. She persisted; she was vastly helpful; and she was always a good sport. Any young woman that could survive this ordeal was made of heroic stuff. In due time she herself was banded. And that was how I trapped my wife. And we have lived happily ever after.

I would advise any young naturalist contemplating matrimony to adopt some such strategy as mine to insure capture of the right mate. The lot of a naturalist's wife is usually rugged; it might as well be so from the very start.

My wife was singularly fortunate in the choice of her forebears. They were pioneers in the best New England tradition; they were all venturesome, independent, and courageous seafaring people. Fear was unknown to them. They were past masters in the art of handling people. So my wife came naturally by her role as the keeper of the gate.

Except for a new paved road which cut through the little village, Drehersville looked unchanged in early September, 1935. We had been away from the mountain since the previous November. The Kochs were unchanged and as jolly as ever. Their greeting could not have been warmer had we been their own children. It was a happy homecoming. Our second season at Hawk Mountain was off to a pleasant and comfortable start. But the mountain road was worse than ever. "The rocky road to Dublin" was a boulevard by comparison. We renewed the "no-trespassing" posters and had a special sign made for the entrance.

We were anxious to obtain a complete day-by-day record of the hawk-flights throughout the season. A numerical study of the migrating *Raptores,* showing the relative frequency of the different species, correlated with the weather and wind conditions, might be of unusual ornithological interest. To do this, however, precluded my spending any time along the road.

The Emergency Conservation Committee had offered me a salary, but the Committee could not again afford to engage a deputy sheriff to patrol the road. Yet someone was needed to stand guard at the Sanctuary entrance, especially on week ends, to deter gunners and to greet our guests, while I served as guide and watcher at the Lookout.

Irma resolved all this by volunteering to be the keeper of

the gate for a few hours each day. I had misgivings about letting a slight little woman, weighing no more than a hundred pounds, stay alone on that lonely mountain road. But she insisted. She had a police whistle which she could use to bring me out of the woods "on the double"—if I heard it. And she had our dog for company.

We had come to Hawk Mountain the year before to protect migrating hawks. Now we were back for the same purpose, simply to protect the hawks, and to learn something about their migration, if possible. We were only vaguely aware that we had also set the stage at Hawk Mountain for a never-ending human drama. People, multitudes of people from all walks of life, were to throng to the Sanctuary from season to season to observe the pageantry of big birds. Our human visitors were to become as much a seasonal pageant as the birds.

Stories about Hawk Mountain, with a friendly, sympathetic slant, began to appear in many local newspapers. A popular columnist of a Philadelphia newspaper referred to Hawk Mountain as "the finest wildlife sanctuary in the State . . . making Drehersville, in Schuylkill County, known all over the United States." We began to enjoy numerous journalistic flights of hyperbole, as well as the flights of hawks. The Drehersville people lapped up the newspaper publicity like kittens at their milk bowl. It was a relief to find that they were no longer openly hostile toward us, as they had been the year before. The "hawk-woman" had a pleasant visit at the gate one afternoon with a group of neighbors from Drehersville, some of them former hawk-shooters who once regarded us as not being quite human. Game Protector Jones, one of the first persons we had met along the road the previous year, made a return visit, almost to the day. I remembered how suspicious, how discouraging, he had been. Now he was cordiality itself.

A Sunday in late September rolled round and, to our amazement, a steady stream of visitors rolled up the road, many of them sightseers who had come to "see what it was all about." Irma found herself directing traffic and advising people where and how to park along the narrow road; this was part of her job every season thereafter. The whistle came in handy. All afternoon she was busy meeting and greeting people, and selling or passing out conservation literature. But she had seen nothing yet! Though more than two hundred grown-ups and children were introduced to Hawk Mountain, the "hawk-woman," and no hawks (for it was an "off day" in the migration), that day was a signpost to the future.

A few sightseers were infuriated with us because of the condition of the road. One man said acidly, "You have no business to advertise in the papers with such a road as this." Irma always explained patiently that we never advertised, that we were not responsible for newspaper publicity about Hawk Mountain. Again and again, my wife had to swallow such grumblings, until by the grace of God the road was improved in the summer of 1939.

The bruised feelings of such individuals usually healed by the time they had reached the relaxed atmosphere of the Lookout. The invigorating climb and the wind-swept rocky pinnacle, offering spectacular vistas, have induced a happy frame of mind in our visitors. There have been, and there always will be, exceptions, however. Through the years some people, returning to the gate, have said to Irma sharply, "You ought to pay us to walk up there!" And there have been the flitter-bugs who, after spending a few minutes at the summit, expecting to see hordes of hawks and eagles, wing to wing, would return and haul my wife over the coals because there were no birds to see. She took it going and coming!

October brought greater throngs of visitors, including a

few hunters. Irma could handle them all. One day as she was knitting at the entrance, a car pulled up with five hunters from Tamaqua, a near-by coal city. The men were redolent of rye—and not the pure grain from the fields! With them were a couple of beagles which slipped off into the woods, pursued by our dog. The men had scarcely noticed the signs; they were not impressed and they were going up the path to shoot hawks anyway. There must have been fire in my wife's eyes, and steel in her words, for presently the men retrieved the dogs, piled into their car and were off. Another time a hunter stood grousing at the gate because Irma did not allow him to shoot at a passing "hawk"—actually only a butterfly!

Irma had a few more encounters like these before the season ended. The men always departed readily, though some accepted her invitation to walk to the Lookout without their guns. I was always glad to receive such individuals at my end, for they were generally receptive to our point of view. Among the latter was a mechanic from Hamburg whose "re-education" was so complete that he became our friend and an able ambassador of hawk protection. A Pottsville merchant, a hater of hawks, came to scoff, but he departed with a new perspective and a handful of our literature on hawks, which he purchased. There was also a young man who spent an entire afternoon; when he left he told me that he had once killed "hundreds of hawks" from these rocks. "Never again," said he, and he meant it, for he often came after that, enjoying each visit tremendously. These men were typical of a small element among the gunners that Irma let pass through the Sanctuary.

We adopted a policy of never preaching hawk protection. If our guests were interested, we would discuss conservation in general and gradually lead up to the many checks and balances in nature. Then we could talk about hawks and other so-called predators.

That season, 1935, the keeper of the gate admitted upwards of 1,250 visitors to the Sanctuary. The three months passed like a pleasant breeze. I had amassed much interesting data on 15,766 hawks and eagles and other birds; and we made many friends for the Sanctuary. What could I do to repay my wife for her devoted and efficient help? All she wanted was a good pair of field glasses, so I bought an 8 x 40 Zeiss binocular. But she never enjoyed it, for in December, while stopping in New York City, en route to Cape Cod, the binocular was stolen from our car.

Since 1935 Irma has been the keeper of the gate on week ends only. The rest of the week she spends recovering from the Sunday irruptions. Each year the Sanctuary gained in popularity. Irma has often found herself playing hostess to as many as 850 visitors on a single Sunday. Saturdays have never been quite so difficult; rarely have more than 100 guests arrived on that day, and they are usually seasoned naturalists, properly dressed, equipped with thermos bottles and lunches, binoculars and every conceivable type of camera.

Newspaper and magazine articles have accounted for the big Sunday influxes. Our Philadelphia columnist, a man of amazing imagination, once wrote in his paper *(The Inquirer),* "It is estimated that 25,000 eagles and their various hawk cousins visit Hawk Mountain in a year. There they rear their young and there they form the best big wild bird show in America." A pleasant week end would bring on a rush of tourists to see this curious spectacle. And if the weather proved too pleasant and mild, the "various hawk cousins" would be conspicuously absent. So poor Irma had to explain to everyone coming along what it was all about, with emphasis on the fact that the hawks did *not* "rear their young" at Hawk Mountain. On such week ends, the cars line up, bumper to bumper, as far down the road as the eye can see, and they bear many out-of-state license plates. And always, on Sundays, people arrive at the entrance until dark, expecting to see hawks.

Many of our automotive mountaineers arrive in their best Sunday clothes, as though they were going to the theatre. And urban women, both delicate and otherwise, come in high heels, or in shoes with the toes sticking out. Irma has counseled thousands of high-heeled women *not* to attempt the rough path that leads to the Lookout, two-thirds of a mile away. Many women, perhaps made heady by the stimulating mountain air, get ambitious and reject any suggestions. So up they go, shoes or no shoes, and it is a miracle how some of these city people get over the rocky path without barking shins or spraining ankles. I once saw a young mother with a three-weeks' old baby at the Lookout, and how she got there was a wonder, for she wore three-inch heels. Many a high-heeler has returned to Irma with ruined shoes and, curiously enough, a sweet temper. The women seldom complain, as do the men who are not used to rugged outdoor exercise. After all, it is the men who must pay for the shoes!

"Are the hawks flying today?" is a question that has been asked at the gate some 30,000 times. On an average Sunday, when five hundred or more people come singly or in small groups, this simple question falls on my wife's ears like a trip hammer. Maybe she'd like to scream, but if the hawking is good, Irma knows it and she steers the visitors up the path quickly with enthusiastic reports. But if the hawking is dull or nil, due to mild weather, Irma's reply may be a laconic, "No hawks, no wind, too warm." One Sunday in 1936, 545 visitors had registered, and by a coincidence we had tallied exactly that many hawks, and everyone was thrilled with the fine show.

"What time do you feed the hawks?" was a frequent question put to Irma in the early days. We do not know how this absurd notion got started, but it was a hard one to crush. Many of our visitors expected to find the hawks and eagles in large cages.

In the autumn of 1938, we began to exact a fifteen cents admission fee from adult visitors, to help defray Sanctuary expenses. Later it became twenty-five cents. You would be surprised to know how many people have tried to slip past my wife without paying! When she has caught such people, she has been far more tactful and patient than ever I would have been. "Well, what do you do with all the money you take in?" ask some. Irma might say, "Do you ask that of the theatre manager every time you go to a movie?" Or she might explain that, in spite of the fact that we are an educational organization, chartered under the laws of the state and exempt from taxation, we nevertheless voluntarily pay taxes, as well as salaries and maintenance expenses. Her category of expenses makes an impressive summary of Sanctuary operation and management. On more than one occasion, the cheeky newcomers have apologized and left a donation to the Sanctuary.

Mrs. Edge told me this story of Irma at the gate: "One afternoon a party of enthusiastic young bird-men arrived in a very fine car. It was their first visit to Hawk Mountain. They eagerly examined our literature, and then each wrote out a slip for membership in our Association. While they were busy, the gilded youth in whose no less gilded car they had arrived, addressed too familiar remarks at and to Irma. She appeared not to notice him; but I was on the point of rebuking him, and only waited because I was curious to see how Irma would handle the situation. The boys each laid down two dollars for annual membership, and the playboy, not to be outdone by his companions, asked for a membership blank. Irma handed him one, merely saying, 'We have

a junior membership for those up to seventeen. It is one
dollar.' Her face was politely serious, but she could not keep
her eyes from laughing. He wrote his name on the slip, laid
down a crisp five-dollar bill and walked soberly, or almost
soberly, up the trail."

During the three years of the war, when I toured the Pacific with the United States Navy, there was no keeper of
the gate, for none was needed, in view of the restrictions of
wartime traveling. Irma waited out the war years for me in
a small New England town, where she was happily employed
in—you may have guessed—public relations work.

I do not think that any wildlife refuge has attracted such
varied human elements as has Hawk Mountain. At the gate
Irma has had a chance to chat with everyone, and her meeting with all kinds of people might well fill an entertaining
book. Have you ever heard of a "needle-straightener"? Well,
they are indispensable people in knitting mills. We had one
as our guest one day. Another time a meek little Italian appeared at the entrance, asking permission to see the "statu-
ary." He turned out to be a stone carver, slightly confused.
Once a very expensive car came along, with a uniformed
chauffeur and an elegantly-dressed, bejeweled woman past
middle age. She proceeded up the path, helped by her chauffeur, and she almost expired at the Lookout. "Too many
cigarettes and too little exercise," the chauffeur confided.

Through all the years people from all over the continent,
and from Newfoundland to Argentina, England to Japan,
have found their way to Hawk Mountain Sanctuary. In the
ten week ends that constitute a hawking season, we have had
an average of 4,500 visitors, many of whom proudly carry
Hawk Mountain Sanctuary Association membership cards.
Teachers and truck drivers, nurses and night-watchmen,
salesmen and scientists, Irma has welcomed them all. To

reach and influence so many diverse types of people has been in itself an extremely rich and rewarding experience.

Many high compliments have been paid to my wife, the best of which I know came from a newsman on the Allentown *Morning Call*. In a generous tribute printed in October, 1947, he summed up my wife and her job perfectly: "Arrivals at the entrance to the Sanctuary are greeted by Irma Broun. She collects the admission fee or checks the credentials. The admission is a quarter for non-members; nothing for members. With the admission goes any and all information the visitor may want. Irma Broun knows all the answers. She gives them in a manner which indicates that she regards it as a privilege to do so. Like all naturalists, she is wholly devoted to the project in hand, and she is a gracious receptionist." I make a bow to my wife Irma, the keeper of the gate.

CHAPTER 5 *SCHOOL*
IN THE CLOUDS

One crisp October day before the war, a group of observers at the Lookout was treated to a remarkable sight. Wide-eyed and astonished, the people saw emerging boldly onto the observation rocks a robust, athletic-looking man, bearing pickaback a man apparently equally robust! Gently, the burden-bearer put his companion down, and soon after we learned that the latter's incapacitation was due to leg injuries sustained in a football game. Anyone who has climbed the rough, two-thirds of a mile footpath from the highway to the mountain summit, can appreciate the truly prodigious feat of strength performed by that Princeton professor—for so he proved to be. Carrying his friend uphill all that distance was eloquent testimony of the lure of Hawk Mountain. I do not recall whether these dauntless men were rewarded with a good flight of hawks; but surely they took with them the memory of the sun-drenched, copper-tinted mountain and, more especially, the spirit of camaraderie of the small gathering of alert, enthusiastic people with whom they were presently fraternizing.

The footpath over which all our visitors must travel to reach the Lookout was once a narrow wagon road. Sixty or more years ago, horse-drawn carts, loaded with sand as nearly fine and snow-white as salt, rumbled down from the great sand quarry almost at the mountain summit. The quarry, long since vested with the green of hemlocks and rhododendrons, is an impressive, hall-like approach to the Lookout. Then for more than a score of years the eroded little cart-path knew only the tread of many hunters who, intent on killing hawks, had turned the mountain to a slaughter pen. Now, in recent years, the path has come to know the tread of more kindly people, sympathetic and *en rapport* with the ways of nature. It has become a nature trail. And the trail tells it story, sometimes amusingly, always informatively.

Every few feet small, unobtrusive signs (some of them painted green to blend with the foliage) tell the story of the woods in pithy phrases. The signs are guide posts to nature. Among the first is one that says: "Twenty kinds of trees common to the Blue Mountains are labeled *for you*." Presently we come upon a black gum, and the bird-minded visitor may wish that he had several of these trees in his back yard, for the label reads: "Thirty-two kinds of birds, including the ruffed grouse and wild turkey, are known to eat the fruit of this tree." Moving along we find the familiar sassafras, with its mitten-shaped leaves, and its sign suggests: "Don't let us confuse you, but it's a fact—this distinctive tree belongs to the laurel family; and the mountain laurel near by belongs to the heath family." Then we learn from the next label: "Along this path you'll find *mountain laurel,* state flower of Pennsylvania; *hemlock,* state tree of Pennsylvania; and *ruffed grouse,* state bird of Pennsylvania. But do not expect to find a label attached to the last item!" Then there are "flop-labels," as one small boy has called them. One of these has this query: "What were the world's first manufacturers of paper?" You pull the string and read on the reverse side of the label: "WASPS were the first manufacturers of paper. The paper is formed from chewed wood. There is a nest in the hemlock, above your head. But wasps do not scatter paper through the woods and along roads, as human beings do. LET US

FOLLOW THE WASPS' EXAMPLE!" And so, from the highway to the Lookout, the very young may run and read, but elderly visitors, pausing to read the labels, find them convenient stopping stations to rest and to regain breath during the ascent to the mountain. Finally, near the end of the trail, we find a message that seems pertinent and timely. It is a quotation from Glenn Frank: "If forests bring health to men's bodies, they also bring beauty to their spirits. A nation that forgets beauty will in time find even the foundation of its technical and economic achievements crumbling."

Bird-students and wilderness-lovers instinctively gravitate to Hawk Mountain. And once "bitten," the Hawk Mountain enthusiast makes at least one pilgrimage annually. The Sanctuary exerts a magnetic appeal. For years a score of members of the Genesee Valley Ornithological Society of Rochester, New York, have journeyed to the Sanctuary to spend a week end in October. Similarly, a delegation of the Schenectady Bird Club has come the long distance to spend a few hours. The Cleveland Bird Club has three times chartered a huge bus for some of its sixty ardent bird-students, who cheerfully endure the rugged 550-mile trip to spend a day and a half on the mountain. And a host of other groups have come regularly, from Buffalo, Cincinnati, Pittsburgh, Wilmington, and Washington, D. C. Dr. John B. May, author of *The Hawks of North America,* has come almost yearly all the way from Boston. Clayton M. Hoff, dynamic executive of the Brandywine Valley Association, one year came from Wilmington, Delaware, on seven Sundays successively. Another man came eighty-five miles every Saturday to see a golden eagle, but without any luck until his seventh visit. Another traveled the three hundred forty miles from Erie, to tell us that we might be mistaken in our identifications of golden eagles, "for the birds simply do not occur in the East!" Scarcely had he voiced his opinion when two golden eagles came into view, both fine adults.

Store clerks and scientists, teachers and farmers, Boy Scouts and Girl Scouts, housewives and their children have hobnobbed on the rocky vantage points. The charms of a variegated, far-spread landscape, the procession of hawks and smaller birds, the keen enjoyment lighting up the faces of these diverse people, all combine to make a unique and inspiring spectacle. The Sanctuary, unknown to the general public before 1934, has since then attracted visitors from places as distant as Switzerland and Japan.

In the late fall of 1946, Dr. William Rhein and Robert Troxel, both of Harrisburg, turned up at the Sanctuary after an absence of four years. Both had been in service in Japan in the early part of that year, and had there met a Japanese friend of Hawk Mountain. When they told me his name, I well remembered how one day in October, 1937, there had appeared at the Lookout an impressively tall young Japanese, Soichiro Ohara, and his petite wife, both of Kurashiki. They were on their honeymoon, and their steamer had scarcely arrived at New York when they engaged a taxi and started for Hawk Mountain! It had been raining, and the mountain road was muddy. The taxi-driver, fearful of getting stuck along the road, would not drive to the gate; after parking the car a half mile or more below the entrance, his passengers tramped the remainder of the way. Mrs. Ohara had her little shoes strapped securely to her ankles, using her silk stockings as straps! Unfortunately they struck a poor flight day, but the Oharas saw a few ospreys, some redtails, and a marsh hawk; and they were profoundly impressed with the scenery, which they compared to a certain locality in Japan. Curiously enough, both Dr. Rhein and Bob Troxel had, independently, the good fortune to meet Ohara, a conservationist who maintains a private experimental station, the Ohara

Institute, at Kurashiki, where he has plant pathologists, ento-
mologists, plant breeders and agronomists in his employ. It
is the only institute of its kind in Japan. Imagine their surprise and pleasure, when Ohara told these men that he had
visited Hawk Mountain.

Time and again I have seen excited new arrivals at the
Lookout greeted by old friends; witnessing this is always a
pleasant experience to me. I shall never forget the delighted
surprise of Mrs. Junea W. Kelley, who had hopped the continent from Alameda, California, in September, 1947, to spend
four exciting days expressly to see "thousands of broad-
wings." She was amply rewarded. And who should happen
along at the same time, westward bound after a summer spent
in upstate New York, but Lloyd Tevis, Jr., a young biologist
from Carmel, California, and an acquaintance of Mrs.
Kelley's! Another time I absorbed some of the spontaneous,
overflowing joy with which two botanists came together at
the Lookout. They had not seen each other since their student days at Cornell, years earlier. Truly, Hawk Mountain
Sanctuary is the crossroads of naturalists.

The day-long passage of hawks is an irresistible attraction.
Given a good flight day, the observers' interest in the show is
unwavering. With binoculars and telescopes ready, competition is keen as to who may see first, and correctly identify,
the oncoming birds as they appear like specks over the distant knobs of the ridge. Newcomers soon learn that these
knobs are numbered from right to left. Throughout the day
there are shouts: "Hawk low over 2"; "Three hawks high
over 4"—and immediately all eyes are riveted to the designated spot; the identity of the traveler is determined long
before it swings its sails past the Lookout. It is a fascinating
sport—and a heartwarming, inspiring sight. As the Baltimore
Sun has observed: "Hundreds find sport with field glasses
where formerly a few dozen gunners wasted shot and flesh."

The change has been the ripening of a rare adventure in conservation.

But there come dull periods or off days when the birds are not flying. The observers gather into small groups, and before you can find a "soft" rock to sit upon there is a discussion going on. Eavesdropping on any one of the gatherings, you are surprised at the range and wealth of the topics discussed. As one young man remarked to me, "Why, it's a liberal education to be up here!" This statement is easily illuminated with a few random gleanings from the lore of the Lookout.

Dr. Ralph W. Stone, a prominent geologist, noticing some curious, intertwining, radiating ridges on a great slab of rock over which people were passing constantly, called his friends together. They were treated to an informal lecture on *Arthrophycus*. To everybody's amazement, they learned that the marks on the rocks represent the fossilized burrowings of a large sea-worm that flourished on the sandy bottom of the Silurian Sea, perhaps one-half billion years ago! Some country people have identified these rock markings as Indian hieroglyphics, while others think that they are inscriptions made by the devil! But it was wonder enough to these people to find that the towering promontory of the mountain on which they stood was once the bottom of a great inland sea.

I remember another fall morning, brilliant but birdless. The Lookout was gay with people clad in bright outdoor clothes and beaming with expectancy. Since the birding proved poor, a young biologist from Ithaca produced a Gray's *Botany,* and the first thing I knew he was surrounded by a small gathering which took a lively interest in identifying some thirty kinds of trees and shrubs that are found at the Lookout. The group was especially interested in a huge, attractive clump of mountain holly *(Nemopanthus mucronata),* which forms the crowning vegetative feature of the Lookout, as the shrub springs directly from clefts in the exposed, barren rocks—a singular occurrence, for the plant's normal habitat is damp, cool woods, often boggy situations, in the mountains of the Northeast.

Do you believe in divining rods? Again at the Lookout I once listened to Devin A. Garrity, the publisher, from New York City, argue persuasively on the efficacy of divining rods. The publisher's friends were skeptical. Along came an Amish woman, clad in typical black bonnet and simple dress. The publisher drew her into the discussion. Yes, she had "known of people" who had used sticks of witch hazel with which to discover water. Then my wife entered the debate, telling how her grandfather had used willow twigs successfully to locate water on his property on Cape Cod. "Some people have the faculty to use divining rods, but many do not," added my wife. On this testimony the publisher's argument ended triumphantly, if not with scientific conclusiveness.

One forenoon the conversation among some Boy Scouts concerned skinks. "Don't you know what a skink is?" asked one boy somewhat haughtily of his companions. No, they did not; they had never heard of a skink, and "there ain't no such critter" implied one. Then I interrupted and said that indeed we had skinks, "right on these rocks, and I'm not referring to anything two-legged." Just then, to my own amazement, a small lizard with a brilliant blue tail came into view from a rock-crevice, announcing itself with a flick of its tongue; it eyed the boys nonchalantly, then disappeared quicker than I could say "I told you so!" It was one of our blue-tailed skinks (Eumeces fasciatus), specimens of which I see but two or three times each season. They are as elusive as will-o'-the-wisps. And our Lookout is the only place in the entire region, apparently, where this lizard has been seen.

Pigeon fanciers, as a group, probably consider all hawks anathema. Not so Dr. T. McKean Downs, a physician from

Philadelphia, who related to us, after witnessing excitedly a peregrine flash by the Lookout at express-train speed, that one of his hobbies was raising fancy pigeons. But another of his hobbies had been falconry. Surely an odd combination, keeping fancy pigeons and hawks! The doctor had a fine, mature goshawk, which now and then managed to capture one of the pigeons. "But that was all right with me," he explained, "because if the pigeon wasn't alert enough to keep out of the way of the hawk, perhaps it needed to be eliminated. *I* wouldn't know which pigeons to eliminate from the flock to keep it up to par."

On another occasion two men stood at the Lookout deploring the gaunt, dead trees that stand out prominently from the forest. This was a new angle to me. Since I was not supposed to be listening, I kept my own counsel, until one of the men turned to me and suggested, "Why don't you cut them down and improve the view?" Improve the view! I was too surprised to say anything, for I had always admired these tree skeletons, so natural and charming a part of the landscape. I paused to edit my thoughts, and then explained that the great dead hemlocks and other trees were relics of a forest fire, due to man's carelessness, that ravaged the area more than thirty years ago. Would they like some exercise? I had two sharp axes at the cottage! "But," I ventured more seriously, "don't you think that the wild character, the picturesqueness of the mountain is enhanced by these former monarchs?" The men were not impressed. "Well, look over there," I said, pointing to an enormous dead hemlock, a large hole near its top. "I happen to know that a pair of flickers raised a family in that hole. And there are many more holes like that, occupied in the summer by chickadees, crested flycatchers, several kinds of woodpeckers, to say nothing of such animals as flying squirrels. Eliminate the dead trees and stumps and you do away with birds which naturally nest in holes in trees. It happens commonly around towns, and then people wonder why insect pests increase. The birds are driven back into the wilderness. Besides furnishing shelter for the birds, these dead trees eventually disintegrate, rot, and form humus." Then I elaborated on the multitude of interdependent life forms which flourish in the humus of the forest floor—the humus which is the core of existence for man and mouse, milliped and moth. Yes, dead trees took on new significance, if not beauty, to these men, who now realized that "improvement" may well mean impoverishment. Time and again at the Lookout, I have found myself giving interested individuals or groups the fundamentals of ecology, or conservation.

Through the years, hundreds, yes *thousands* of visitors have heard our "sermons on the mount"—informal talks, sometimes special talks, about the Sanctuary, or aspects of conservation, or perhaps the geological interpretation of the landscape. Often, should the hawks put on a show, my "sermons" are interpolated with hasty comments on hawk identification. I have addressed such varied groups as Seventh Day Adventists, Isaac Waltonians, hiking clubs, professors from a New York university, ornithological societies, women's garden and church clubs, third-grade rural school children, and many Scouts. Scout groups, boys and girls, have been my most numerous listeners. During one season more than eight hundred Scouts visited the Sanctuary, and I talked to more than half of them. Once, after I had talked to some thirty Girl Scouts—and showed them two golden eagles—one of the leaders of the group, a clergyman from a near-by town, confided to me that once upon a time he had been among those misguided persons who had slaughtered the hawks from these very rocks. Now, he and his wife were delighted to have their charges learn the truth about hawks and their place in nature's complex pattern.

Who could have anticipated, when the Sanctuary was founded, all the glad and exciting hours that many people have enjoyed here? What a surprising chain of events was set in motion when Mrs. Edge birthed her unique project by taking over an entire mountaintop to protect the migrating hawks. It is pleasant to look down the vista of the years to 1934. We embarked on a precarious venture, in an undeveloped area, among people few of whom showed any sympathy for hawk protection. Our trials were many. Now, most of the residents of our region are proud of the unique institution in their midst that has attracted thousands of visitors each fall. An editorial about the Sanctuary in the Allentown *Morning Call,* October 26, 1946, begins, "There are thousands of naturalists throughout the United States who envy the naturalists in this part of the country because almost at our back door is one of the greatest places for wild birds in the United States, namely Hawk Mountain." A glowing contrast to the newspaper article quoted in our first chapter, on page 8.

Many parks and refuges have brought unsuspected economic blessings to their communities, largely through catering to tourists. Formerly, tourists were unknown in the region of Hawk Mountain. But almost from its inception the Sanctuary has brought to the community each fall a hitherto undreamed-of revenue. One farmer's wife, for example, through the excellence of her accommodations and the warmhearted hospitality of her household, has harvested each season between two and three hundreds dollars in clear profit. About once each year we are approached by serious people who would like to establish a refreshment stand at the gate! Hotels, any number of tourist homes, and filling-stations, have benefited substantially. Thus the swarms of bird-lovers and conservationists have demonstrated that there is more pleasure and profit at Hawk Mountain with cameras and binoculars than there had been in the earlier days with guns. Almost any week end there are among the visitors at the Lookout men who will admit having taken part in the hawk-shoots of earlier years.

Prior to 1946, the Sanctuary was open to the public only during the three months that cover the autumn migration of hawks. The resources of the Sanctuary could not stretch further. We counted more friends than dollars. During the war years the Directors, with care and economy, put aside money with which to operate the Sanctuary the year round, for how long depends on popular support. Scout groups, hiking clubs, garden clubs, and other groups come regularly to the Sanctuary during the spring and summer to avail themselves of the Sanctuary's excellent camping facilities and to enjoy informally conducted nature tours and talks.

Thus the Sanctuary has advanced far beyond its original goal of protecting the migrating hawks. In the beginning it was apparent that the public welcomed and appreciated this bold, pioneering stroke. The fact of active hawk protection, a desire so long thwarted in those who knew best the value of the hawks, drew the nature-minded people. Astonishment that people would want to protect hawks drew hundreds of others, who welcomed information, enjoyed the mountain and contact with enthusiastic outdoor people.

It is not the multitudes of hawks that pass the Lookout on Hawk Mountain that is so important, although people in ever-increasing numbers travel from all parts of America to watch them. It is what the Sanctuary stands for and the influence for good that it is having on the popular imagination. The Sanctuary has been the subject of hundreds of newspaper and magazine articles. Such varied publications as *Time Magazine, Pageant, The Spur, Holiday, Natural History, Nature Magazine,* and the *International Journal of Animal Protection* of Scotland, have featured the work and the purpose of Hawk Mountain. Among the nicest compliments that the Sanctuary has enjoyed have been a half dozen invitations from radio stations, to spread its story and its message over the nation's airways. One fall a party of naturalists from the Staten Island Museum spent a week end at the Lookout making sketches and plans for a diorama of the mountain and the birds of prey. Thus Hawk Mountain in miniature has been displayed at this museum and in the American Museum of Natural History, and elsewhere. Movie audiences from coast to coast have also seen the Sanctuary in technicolor, in a recreational film which was produced and distributed before the war, by the Pennsylvania Department of Publicity and Information.

Best of all, in June, 1937, reacting favorably to our pioneering in hawk protection, the Pennsylvania Game Commission extended protection to all the hawks, except the goshawk, the sharp-shinned and the Cooper's hawks. We do not consider this adequate, however. But it does represent a great advance for a state whose game commission had hitherto been notoriously hostile or indifferent toward hawks and owls. The inability of the average hunter to distinguish between a Cooper's hawk and a red-shouldered hawk, especially if the latter species is in immature plumage, and the five-dollar bounty on the rare goshawk (which most sportsmen and many bird students cannot tell from any other hawk), thus making most hawks potential victims of the bounty, point up the weaknesses of Pennsylvania's hawk protection laws. Protection, with penalty by fine, should be accorded *all* hawks and owls. Only when a bird is caught red-handed in the act of damaging property should it be destroyed.

Hawk Mountain Sanctuary Association was a natural and inevitable blossoming from an inspired idea. The Association, like the Sanctuary, was brought into being by Mrs.

Edge. The Association was incorporated in Pennsylvania in 1938, at which time Mrs. Edge deeded to it the 1401 acres that comprise the Hawk Mountain property. The money for the purchase of the property, and the money that had supported the Sanctuary during the years prior to 1938, was generously given by loyal conservationists, through the Emergency Conservation Committee, which had sponsored the project. The object of this association is "To create a sympathetic understanding for birds and wild life, to provide means of educating the public thereto," and to protect, encourage and permit to live without molestation *all* wild life within the Sanctuary.

The Sanctuary is maintained through the faithful support of almost 1300 Hawk Mountaineers—our members, who are scattered in forty-three states, Canada, Mexico, Venezuela and Hawaii. About half of these people are residents of Pennsylvania; about three-fifths of our members are men. The Sanctuary activities and affairs are directed by a Board of Directors, from which four officers are elected. Mrs. Edge, ever an alert and vivid personality, a natural leader of conservationists, has been a pillar of Hawk Mountain Sanctuary Association, serving as its president since the start. Four classes of membership, beginning with an annual membership at two dollars, have been open to all who are in sympathy. By means of newsletters, distant members are kept in touch with all that goes on at the Sanctuary. The people who are concerned about the Sanctuary, who take an active, affectionate interest in it, come from all walks of life; they include poultry-raisers and physicians, housewives and horticulturists, two or three admirals and a celebrated actress.

It was the veteran naturalist, the late Vernon Bailey, who inspired this chapter heading. He wrote to Mrs. Edge in October, 1941: "I must tell you how much the twenty members of the Washington, D. C., Audubon Society enjoyed

Hawk Mountain last Sunday; not only the hawks but the scenery, the autumn colors, the plants and geology, and especially the people. The well-labeled nature trail would be a credit to our National Parks. . . . I want to congratulate you on having started this school in the clouds that is reaching so far and so many."

I like to think of the Sanctuary as just that, a "school in the clouds," where one sees and learns about nature by association, in an effortless manner; where knowledge of nature is tempered with humor, kindled with good fellowship, sparked by the inspiration of many inquiring minds and kindred spirits, whose common ideal is the simple creed: "Live and let live."

CHAPTER 6

SANCTUARY—
WE MEAN IT!

A number of years ago W. L. McAtee, dean of wildlife biologists, clarified the meaning and significance of sanctuaries in an essay called *Sanctuary—Do We Mean It?* published and distributed by the Emergency Conservation Committee. Because it defines the problems so lucidly and sums up exactly our own philosophy of what constitutes a sanctuary, it is pertinent to quote a few paragraphs:

"The term 'sanctuary' has a traditional meaning that is unequivocal, but in modern parlance it may signify a variety of things, among which perhaps the last is that of a place of refuge for all wild life. . . .

"The true nature lover prizes all living things and will not be a party to the absurd doctrine that a bird sanctuary must be kept clear of certain birds as the Cooper's and sharp-shinned hawks or the screech owls. The nature lover, furthermore, will not subscribe to the dictum that a refuge without interference by man becomes a paradise for so-called 'vermin.' This claim is not only unacceptable to the general conservationist on principle but is untrue. . . .

"A great need is for more wild-life reservations, where the compact with Nature implied in the term 'sanctuary' will be fully observed both in letter and in spirit."

We subscribe to these principles one hundred per cent. When we saw Hawk Mountain Sanctuary, *we mean it!*

There are many kinds of sanctuaries, and all manner of policies governing their management. Many a sanctuary suffers from "developments" which detract from what should be its true purpose: the restoration or preservation of the natural habitat.

I once knew a misguided refuge manager who enthusiastically set about building ski-runs within his reservation, which is all right only if the object is a sanctuary for skiers. Another obnoxious kind of "sanctuary" is the one where wildlife is exploited as an exhibit—in order to profit from tourists. In New England I know of a small, fenced-in, well-groomed "sanctuary," where semi-domestic mallards and Canada geese are pampered, and all owls, hawks, foxes and other predacious creatures are shot on sight—a deplorable situation typical of many sanctuaries where preferential treatment is accorded certain types of birds and mammals. I have no patience and less use for such "sanctuaries." I will admit that control or restrictive measures are sometimes needed, but only under the most careful, expert supervision, while indiscriminate elimination of any native wildlife is never justifiable.

At Hawk Mountain all wildlife is inviolate; the fox is as welcome as the deer; our great horned owls are appreciated and respected as much as the grouse. Wildlife management, in my opinion, should mean stringent protection of the wildlife, and letting nature alone to work out her own checks and balances. The only creature that I have found necessary to restrict in numbers is the pilot black snake. While admittedly a valuable rodent-catcher, this reptile, if too numerous, becomes a serious menace to nesting birds. Hence, around our Sanctuary headquarters, where every effort is made to encourage birds, I have had to remove black snakes.

The basic requirements for any true sanctuary for wildlife, large or small, are simple. They involve clearly-defined boundaries which must be well posted against hunting; active, vigilant watchfulness against poaching; and supervision with as little human interference as possible. Certain other requirements should be met: dead trees must not be removed —the forest dwellers make them into homes; fires should be strictly taboo except in designed areas; footpaths for human visitors should never be too numerous, nor should they penetrate into the choicest areas for wildlife; wild nuts and fruits belong to the wildlife of the sanctuary; and, finally, no flowers or other plants should be touched. Hawk Mountain Sanctuary meets all these requirements, especially as regards the boundaries, which are well brushed and defined with a strand of wire.

With the advent of the deer-hunting season in early December, and tremendous hunting pressure in the lowlands, the deer, followed by the hunters, swarm over the Blue Mountains. And at this season more and more deer crowd into the Sanctuary; the only thing that saves them is our strand of wire, with the prominently displayed posters proclaiming the area a *wildlife refuge*. Local hunters seemed unable to comprehend the word *Sanctuary*, which was printed on our posters in the first few years. We had trouble. But the hunters have reacted well to the word *refuge*, combined with a wire. The State game refuges are enclosed with a strand of wire, and the Pennsylvania hunters have learned to respect a wire. Many local farmers and hunters, who were once openly hostile toward the Sanctuary, now indorse it, realizing that the deer and other game that we protect will renew themselves and repopulate the countryside.

The Sanctuary is spread over 1401 acres of wild, rugged terrain. It takes in a bit of the Little Schuylkill River, at 550 feet above sea level, and reaches upwards a thousand feet to the Lookout, to a whole series of exposed rock promontories (the former hawk-shooting stands), and to an extensive plateau that fades toward the south. There is a sad melody in the little river, which moves in stricken, funereal slowness along the base of the mountain; the river is biologically dead, clogged with silt and sulphurous wastes from the coal regions. During the past two years this river, "one of the world's most degraded streams," has been subjected to an intensive program of reclamation. It is estimated that the project, when completed, may cost upwards of fifty-five million dollars.

A mixed growth of birches, oaks, hemlocks, white and pitch pines, and great tangles of mountain laurel and rhododendron are the dominant forest constituents. Among the animals that find cover, food and homes within the Sanctuary are salamanders (several kinds) and skinks, raccoons and 'possum, cave rats and three species of shrews including that mammalian Lilliput, the masked shrew (about ten of which would be needed to make an ounce). We have identified 185 species of birds in or flying over the refuge. Our permanent residents include two pairs of pileated woodpeckers, a pair of great horned owls, and many ruffed grouse which find ideal range conditions. Though seasonally we may have a tremendous influx of human visitors, the wildlife is not disturbed; for our human visitors use only two areas: the trail that leads directly from the public road to the Lookout, and a small camping-picnic area near the Sanctuary headquarters. This latter area contains our shelters, stone fireplaces, picnic tables and benches, necessary sanitary facilities, and plenty of pure spring water.

There are days during the magical seasons of migration when Hawk Mountain is fabulously alive with birds. But in the summer, the mountain can be a rather quiet place, with only thirty-five kinds of nesting birds. No great numbers of songbirds can be expected to frequent a densely wooded, rocky upland like Hawk Mountain. However, we have had an exciting adventure demonstrating that a songbird population may be increased under apparently unsuitable conditions. At our Sanctuary headquarters on the east side of the mountain, at 1100 feet, an old apple orchard, gardens and a tiny pasture combine to make the only break in the forest cover for many miles. Few birds frequented the area (three acres) when it was added to the Sanctuary, by purchase, in 1938. To make this area as attractive as possible to birds became a challenge. We provided feeding stations, we introduced a variety of native shrubs that would give birds both food and cover, we erected bird houses, and built brush-piles. And the birds have responded. In the summers of 1947 and 1948, there lived in and about the edges of this three-acre clearing thirty-six birds of fifteen species. Chipping sparrows topped the list, with three pairs, each with a nest (lined with goat hair) in an apple tree.

Twenty-five species of birds, some of them rare visitants to our mountain, have enjoyed our bounty.[1] This does not include the ruffed grouse which we often see within sixty feet of the house, feeding on wild grapes. The red fox and raccoon are also attracted to the great tangles of wild grape, to our deep satisfaction but to the dismay of our querulous though innocuous Cocker spaniels. Of wild grapes there is such an abundance that my wife and I feel that we are entitled to some—just enough to make a few jars of jelly to carry the flavor of summer through the long winters.

[1] Mourning doves
Hairy woodpeckers
Downy woodpeckers
Crow
Black-capped chickadees
Red-breasted nuthatches
House wrens
Catbirds
Robins
Ruby-crowned kinglet
Maryland yellow-throat
Cowbirds
Indigo buntings

Towhees
Savannah sparrows
Vesper sparrows
Slate-colored juncos
Tree sparrows
Chipping sparrows
Field sparrows
White-crowned sparrows
White-throated sparrows
Fox sparrows
Lincoln's sparrows
Song sparrows

A pair of savannah sparrows, quite out of place, once spent an entire day with us. It is doubtful that we would have enjoyed their presence, or the visits of such uncommon guests as white-crowned and Lincoln's sparrows, had we not induced them to "drop in" at our well-stocked food stations. Through bird banding we have determined, among other things, how long our guests tarry. Some of our migrating juncos and tree sparrows have lingered five to seven weeks. In May, indigo buntings flock to our food trays, and six or eight buntings at once make a lively, never-to-be-forgotten picture. The honors for the most unexpected bird to seek our largesse go to a certain crow. I looked out of our living-room window one cold afternoon in May and, to my astonishment, there in the lilacs, only fifteen feet from the window, was the big, sable creature, confidently devouring chunks of suet that had been tied there. All our birds are sure of a square meal at any time, and they have no dishes to wash to earn it, either!

Attracting large numbers of songbirds through artificial feeding poses a real responsibility for their safety from predators. The brush-piles, supplementing the natural cover, insure maximum safety for our charges. One April day, a sharp-shinned hawk flashed across the back yard, twisting and turning in hot pursuit of a small bird which dived safely into one of the brush-piles. When the hawk had passed on, the brush-pile blossomed out with a score of twittering white-throats and juncos. Brush-piles can be truly beautiful!

High up on the mountain, in a secluded hemlock grove about a half mile from our headquarters, there lives each spring and summer a pair of sharp-shinned hawks—the bane of songbirds! But the sharp-shins and their young have our blessings. Fifteen kinds of songbirds live in the neighborhood of the sharp-shins' aerie; yet I have been unable to detect any decrease in their numbers, which represent a normal, balanced population. From the peaceful hemlocks any June day float the dreamy notes of four or five black-throated green warblers; tanagers and indigo buntings flaunt their bright colors among the exposed stubs; and cuckoos move noiselessly among the hemlock boughs. From the sharp-shin's nest we have taken the remains of black and white warblers, black-billed cuckoos, and cardinals, the latter having been obtained from the farmlands more than two miles distant, for no cardinals live on the mountain. Far ranging are the small hawks in quest of their victims: birds which nature intended for removal for sound biological reasons. We do not condemn the sharp-shins, which have as much right to their cuckoos and cardinals as we have to our chicken dinners.

The sharp-shins have lived in this hemlock grove for countless centuries; we hope they will continue to dwell here. We can trace their ancestry back a million years, along with many of the smaller birds. Yet there are altogether too many people who, assuming to possess more wisdom than the Creator, would disrupt this relationship by eliminating the sharp-shins. At Hawk Mountain the little hawks are a symbol of our pact with nature. When we say *Sanctuary, we mean it!*

CHAPTER 7

THE FAR-
SPREAD LAND

From the Lookout of Hawk Mountain, 1521 feet above sea level, spreads one of the most spectacular and most photographed views in Pennsylvania. Under ideal conditions, one's eyes sweep over a seventy-mile expanse of land carved in curious parallel ridges, canoe-shaped valleys, forest and farmland, interspersed with tiny villages whose houses are mere specks in the landscape. And there is not a billboard in sight!

It is indeed a magnificent panorama that the sightseer beholds. However, some people see nothing at all, though they may be blessed with perfectly good eyes. Time and again I have seen people pick their way across our skyline, then stop and stare into space. "Well, what is there to see?" they ask, and presently they disappear down the trail.

Each of us will see the landscape differently and interpret it according to his own lights. The bird watcher has a special interest in our ridge, the salient feature of the land. For the Kittatinny Ridge (the "endless mountain" of the Indians) is a highway over which, in the appointed seasons, pass vast numbers of migrating birds. The naturalist sees the varied terrain as a showcase of plants and animals of two or three overlapping life zones, with the mountain summits containing elements of the Canadian fauna. A conservationist contemplates the forest and sees other values; if wisely managed the forest will provide abundant lumber; it will hold back melting snows and absorb the rains and help temper the climate; and it provides homes for myriad life-forms, from bacteria to deer, whose complex, interdependent lives combine in the end to make human lives supportable. The recreation-seeker looks upon the hills as a natural playground in which he may find health of body and mind and spirit—a means to more creative living. The poet is moved with "a sense sublime" as his vision dwells on the Joseph's coat of green and brown, gold and tan—a symphony of color welling up from the eye-filling architecture of the hills and valleys. To the geologist, the far-spread land is like an open book—a book packed with drama, whose pages speak eloquently yet humbly of the earth's immeasurable past.

The "eternal hills" are but temporal products of the immensity of time. "Time," as one student of earth history has said, "is one of the most overwhelming resources of our universe." And time brings change, be it ever so gradual or imperceptible to human eyes. To comprehend the remote and misty past of the earth, we must, like the astronomer, stretch our mental horizons millions of years. We must take into account all the physical and geological processes which were required to transform our barren globe into a home for countless organisms, including man. Men of science are generally agreed that our earth, born of the sun, is about two billion years old, notwithstanding the laborious calculations of the Bishop Ussher, who decided the world had been created on October 9, 4004 B.C. The slow, vast processes of life are plainly revealed in the rocks, with their fossil records of bacteria and brachiopods, starfish and snails, forming a picture which holds our imagination captive. As we observe this unfolding drama of life, from lowest forms to man, we find that man himself appears only in the last minute of geological time.

Hawk Mountain stands at the crossroads of time. Within the "seventy-mile expanse" of our view lie rocks of all geological ages. As one scans the far horizon toward the southeast, the New Jersey uplands and the rolling hills of Lehigh County (Pennsylvania) form a backdrop to the colorful expanse of the Great Valley just south and east of our ridge. Of pre-Cambrian origin, the distant hills contain some of the oldest known rocks. Formed approximately a billion years ago, when the earth's sole life-matter expressed itself in protoplasmic forms, these faintly visible uplands of gneiss and granite may represent the remnants of *Appalachia*. This, the geologists tells us, was the continental land mass which sloped out into the Atlantic some two hundred miles beyond its present coast-line. Westward from Appalachia rolled a shallow sea, a titanic trough that extended deep into the interior of North America, and from Alabama north to the ancient core of our continent—the Laurentian Shield of Canada. So, in the beginning, the familiar physiographical features upon which the eyes rest at Hawk Mountain were non-existent—literally "without form and void," for the ridge was once at the bottom of the sea.

During an eternity reckoned in millions of years, chemical changes and the forces of erosion gouged vast quantities of rocks from Appalachia. Slowly, ever so slowly, our shallow inland sea filled up with sediments from the eroding landmass. The floor of the Great Valley is made up of limestones, shales and sandstones that were laid down in Cambro-Ordovician times, about a half billion years ago. This is really a very brief period of time compared with the countless eons that went before, eons of preparation and organization for the ever-growing procession of new life-forms. This shallow sea was a laboratory in which were perfected the earliest invertebrates: trilobites, shellfish and coral. In parts of the Valley are exposed fossiliferous beds containing abundant evidence of the marine fauna of those remote times. The sediments of ancient Appalachia have been the very marrow of modern man's culture and existence. For these sediments have given man his slate, cement and lime industries, as well as lead, zinc, iron ores, and other minerals.

Out of the debris of Appalachia also came the sandstone which forms the backbone of our Kittatinny Ridge. The bleached and lichen-covered boulders of the Lookout originated as coarse sediments in Silurian times (when fishes became common) some four hundred million years ago. Many of the solid, attractive farmhouses of our Pennsylvania Dutch neighbors are made from this coarse, granular sandstone.

Immediately to the north of the Lookout, the rocky wall of the mountain tumbles sharply a thousand feet, to the Schuylkill Valley. The richly fossiliferous shales of this valley are identified with the Devonian period, which lasted fifty million years, and gave rise to the first amphibians. Far toward the northeast rise the Poconos, the sandstone strata of which were also laid down during Devonian times. Looming beyond the Schuylkill Valley are the coal fields, visible as far as the eye can see as prominent parallel ridges. They represent the Carboniferous Age of two hundred fifty million years ago. So, in one sweep of the vision we take in the whole of that vast geological segment of time known as the Paleozoic.

Throughout Paleozoic times our Appalachian highland was being attacked and worn down by lashing wind and water. Great rivers flowing down from this land mass discharged debris into the Appalachian trough, filling it with sediments which hardened into rock by the pressure of overlying materials. Time and again these rock strata sank from the tremendous weight, or they became locally altered by being folded and faulted. In the main, the area became a low, undulating plain over which the sea alternately advanced (spreading sand and gravel and clay) or withdrew.

During the last stages of the Paleozoic, a vast forested swamp took form, near sea level—another experimental laboratory. Here were compounded the most astonishing assortment of plants the world has known: tree ferns (they still flourish in tropic regions), giant horsetails, tree-like club mosses that grew to heights of eighty feet or more, and many other types. The partial decomposition and compression of the luxuriant, vigorous vegetation of those times have provided us with coal, petroleum and gas. We might remember that each foot of coal represents the vegetal accumulation of three hundred years. The tropical swamps of the Carboniferous Age lasted about one hundred fifteen million years. They disappeared at times into the sinking earth, to be buried under avalanches of mud, only to spring up again in new forests—a miracle of reincarnation which was repeated more than one hundred times, judging from the number of Pennsylvania coal-beds. So in the last scenes of the Paleozoic, our once shallow inland sea had filled up with successive layers of rock and coal.

Paleozoic time ended about one hundred seventy-five million years ago with the "Appalachian Revolution"—the most stupendous physical disturbance of all geological time. But the change was not cataclysmic; rather it was imperceptibly slow, requiring millions of years. The earth's crust became warped and twisted. A tremendous horizontal pressure from the southeast—geologists have been unable to account for it—now pushed the newly-formed layers of rock and coal northwestward against the anchored wall of the old Laurentian Shield. Dr. George H. Ashley has given us an excellent analogy of this movement in his *Syllabus of Pennsylvania Geology*: "Imagine twenty or thirty long rugs on the floor, one on top of another, and then getting down on your knees and begin-

ning to push one end of the pile, the other end being against
a wall. The folds made in the rugs would resemble those
made in the rock strata of the earth's crust." Thus the vast
layers of rock were raised, broken, and buckled into gigantic
folds projecting a mile or more above sea level. The carboniferous beds of rock and coal became entirely eroded in
the Great Valley during the ensuing ages, but they are preserved in the areas to the north of the Lookout by having
been more strongly downfolded there. At the close of Paleozoic time, therefore, the Appalachian region of today was
a land of mountain peaks resembling the Alps or the Andes.

During the subsequent one hundred million years of the
Mesozoic (when dinosaurs and pterodactyls were the lords of
creation), the towering crests of the new peaks were again
reduced and worn away by the destructive forces of the
weather. The sea had long since withdrawn permanently.
Into the intermontanic hollows the streams poured vast quantities of sand and gravel and clay. These are the Triassic
sediments, preserved locally only eight miles southeast of
Hawk Mountain, on the isolated, eleven-hundred-foot peak
of the "Spitzenburg." The close of the Mesozoic was marked
entirely by erosion and by the appearance of the large land
animals.

At length the entire region, from the Alleghany plateau
to the Atlantic, was reduced to a flat plain sloping gently to
the sea. This was known as the Schooley Peneplain. Remnants of this peneplain are found in many parts of the present-day Appalachians; an especially good example is the
broad, flat summit of the ridge to the south of the Lookout.
On the sloping surface of this peneplain were born the Delaware, the Lehigh, the Schuylkill and the Susquehanna Rivers.
The winds, the rains and these rivers carved valleys out of the
softer rocks, while resistant layers, such as sandstone, granite
and gneiss, stood out prominently, becoming the hills and

mountains of today. And across the mountain the larger streams cut their channels, thus forming the water gaps that have had such an important role in the industrial development of the region.

As is well known, the most recent full-scale geological transformations were wrought during the Ice Age, which began about a million years ago, about the time that primitive man appeared, in the Old World. The fascinating story of the glacial era, and of the discovery of man's bones mingled with the bones of extinct animals, has filled many books. Although only the northern fringe of our "seventy-mile expanse" was touched by the chill fingers of the Ice Age (the complete absence of natural lakes in our immediate landcape makes that abundantly plain), the entire region was profoundly, permanently influenced. Hawk Mountain lies some thirty miles south of the last glacial drifts of thirty-five to forty thousand years ago. In those times the plants that filled our landscape were quite different from those we see today. A timber wolf at the Lookout would have gazed out over an unbroken, dark green mantle of fir and spruce trees stretching to the farthermost horizons. Although climatic conditions are now vastly different (except during certain winters!), relics of that boreal flora may still be found, existing precariously on the higher, north-facing slopes of our mountains. At least one of these hand-downs from the Ice Age (the long beech fern) grows on Hawk Mountain as well as in Greenland.

Our all too-rapid journey through the countless yesteryears has provided us with only the most fleeting glimpses of their living forms. Nature, experimenting ceaselessly, molded and perfected and then discarded one dynasty of plants and animals after another, in favor of better creations. And the story is far from finished. Turning from the long perspective of the geologic past, we can only guess as to the future. Man, though perched momentarily on the top rung of the evolutionary ladder, faces an uncertain future on his heritage of the earth—his already "plundered planet." It is entirely conceivable that our land may again sink below sea level, or appear like "Greenland's icy mountains." One authority claims that the United States is shrinking at the rate of approximately six thousand four hundred acres a year. A minor change of climate could affect man's security and alter his destiny more speedily than any other basic geologic agency. It is interesting to speculate on what might happen to man if the annual average temperature of the earth were to rise only 10° and remain so indefinitely. Such a change would automatically unlock the frozen wastes of the polar regions; the resulting expansions of the oceans would inundate the seaboard cities of the world and obliterate many of its fertile valleys.

Certainly man, the chief wonder of nature's current creations, is doing his best to aid and accelerate nature's processes of change—and extinction. That man himself is a geologic force the world over—and much to his sorrow—has been made abundantly clear in modern times. Consider the five and a half million tons of earth that pass down the Potomac each year; that is a mere trickle compared with the man-caused siltation along the larger waterways of the world. Extraordinary and often violent changes can be charged to the hand of man, during only the past two centuries, in the microcosm of our "seventy-mile expanse."

On page one of a schoolbook published locally in 1916 (*The Story of Berks County*, by Wagner, Balthaser and Hoch) we read: "Two hundred years ago . . . [Berks County] was the home of wild animals and savage Indians. Great forests of giant trees were found in its valleys and on most of its rugged hills. *What wonderful changes we now see!* The forests have nearly all been cut down . . . the savage Indians and wild animals are no longer seen; in their places we have civilized people. . . ." (The italics are mine). Yes, the Red Man is gone, and gone in their entirety are the giant trees. And for better or for worse, most of the wild animals have been forced into extinction. Of the twenty-four animals larger than gray squirrels which lived in Penn's Woods along with the Indians for many centuries, only ten have survived locally. Gone forever are some of the birds, and many kinds of fishes. If that is "progress," we cannot help but wonder who is the "savage"—the Indian, who was adjusted to his environment, or his successor?

From the Lookout our landscape spreads secure and happy and meltingly beautiful in the soft light of a slightly-clouded sky. But if we dare to scrutinize our microcosm with an imaginary magnifying glass, we discover at once much that is sick and shockingly off balance.

The dark little river (the Schuylkill) that threads its serpentine course from the north and skirts the foot of the mountain—the most significant stream in our area—what of it? Once the wood duck and the great blue heron made it their home; shad and trout and a host of other aquatic forms abounded; and it was a wellspring of life to otters and beavers. Under the stewardship of civilized man the little river became a sewer. Along its black Stygian course are borne sulphuric wastes and refuse from the coal regions; Norway rats have replaced all the other creatures. Yet such is the ingenuity of man that these same poisonous waters, through complicated and expensive mechanical processes, are rendered harmless and potable to a huge urban population. This little river typifies what has happened to nearly every large river, and most smaller ones, in the East. Measures have finally been taken, here and there, and at enormous cost to taxpayers, to correct this sad situation. But what of the vanished wildlife? Let the ever-increasing army of hunters ponder why there is not more game. ...

A few miles to the north, in the coal regions, our magnifying glass reveals enormous, deeply-cut scars in the earth; the raw earth is upturned in piles much higher than the average-sized house. These are the strippings which pockmark the anthracite regions. Every last chunk of coal is being scraped and scratched and shoveled up from the surface of the agonized outraged earth—miles and miles of it. The end product of man's labors are prodigious pits which remind us of the craters of the moon. We look about and wonder where a rabbit may hide. We wonder what kind of people, if any, may be able to sustain themselves in this blighted region a few decades hence.

And then, in the distant Pocono plateau, dotted with glacial ponds, we discover the last remnants of the fresh-water fauna which once could be found at the foot of our mountain. Even here man's peculiar lunacy continues to express itself in active warfare against the handful of harmless creatures—herons, kingfishers, water snakes, ospreys and otters—that subsist on fish, yet actually aid man to achieve superior fishing. The Pocono waters are notoriously overpopulated with stunted and worthless fish, due to the removal of the natural predators of fish. Instead of killing all fish-eating animals and birds, instead of extensive (and expensive) restocking, all that is needed is a sane policy of letting nature alone to manage her own affairs.

What of the green mantle of trees that covers our Kittatinny Ridge and the adjoining ridges? At one time or another, every last acre of forest has been "mined" and then ravaged by fires, some often deliberately set by men who were interested only in the profits from "huckleberries." Given time, much time, and freedom from fire and the ruthless buzz saw, the present regenerated forest may yet recapture a little of its former glory. But among the trees, the chestnut, once the most prized of our native forest trees, and certainly of vital importance as a source of food for wildlife, survives only as pathetic sprouts which eventually yield to the dread Asiatic fungus that found its way to our shores in 1904. Now *Anthracnos,* another lethal fungus disease, threatens a whole group of trees—the oaks. Many other native trees seem to be falling by the wayside, from infestations of insects, fungus or the like. Perhaps the lack of soil, or the deterioration of the soil, depriving the more complex plants of essential mineral elements, has weakened their resistance. In any event, we have all these "wonderful changes," and more, in the short space of less than two hundred years. Typical again is this picture of what we find projected on a world-wide scale, while man deplores the scarcity of newsprint, of fuel-oil, of fish, of this and that, and moans the high cost of salmon, of building materials, of keeping alive!

The farmlands, from which the forests have been removed so that men may eat—do they not hold promise? Perhaps, and we truly hope so. Agronomists have performed miracles on the most exhausted soils. Our magnifying glass shows only a few local farms that operate scientifically, to produce maximum yields. The shale and limestone, once thickly carpeted with the humus of great forests, are now conspicuous on eroded, worn-out fields throughout the Great Valley. In spite of farm bureaus and soil administration agencies, we see little contour plowing or strip farming on the open, rolling fields. And more exasperating yet to the lover of the land is the lack of hedgerows, any kind of thickets, on the broad expanses of the distant farmlands. "Clean" farming is the thing in most parts of our tidy Pennsylvania Dutch land. And since many farms lack cover, they also lack quail and the abundance of songbirds that should be present to combat insect pests. The farmers shower their orchards and their crops with insecticides, effectively destroying not only the bugs, both good and bad, but very often killing desirable insect-eating birds as well.

Where the Indian stalked deer and bear, modern man in his expensive hunting regalia has stiff competition searching for introduced pheasants, introduced rabbits, and introduced deer. Native deer became extinct locally before the turn of the century. Introduced deer from Michigan have not only maintained themselves but have increased astonishingly in our newly forested ridges and in the wooded parts of the valleys. Also encouraging is the present abundance of native ruffed grouse in the wooded uplands.

As the face of the land (under our magnifying glass) is tired and harassed, here as elsewhere, wherever man has "conquered his environment," so do we see harassment written on the faces of many of our human visitors to the Lookout. It is symptomatic of our weary, troubled times and of the endlessly vexatious problems that beset man—the new geologic force. Invariably he turns his face to nature for comfort, for peace, and for the inspiration which will give him renewed strength and courage.

Our so-called civilization, materialistic, insatiable, endlessly expanding, is constantly threatening wildlife and its environment, the very values to which man so frequently looks for regeneration of his spirit. Never in the history of man has the need been more urgent for conservation of natural resources, for the perpetuation of our remaining wildlife, and for the preservation of beautiful, primitive areas. Small sanctuaries like Hawk Mountain should be established throughout the country so that all types of ecological niches might be preserved and used as instruction centers. Many garden clubs and natural history groups have already taken such steps. Theirs is a splendid opportunity. But a start only has been made. Far more sanctuaries should be created, with the utmost speed, before it is too late.

How will things look from our Lookout a few centuries hence? Who knows—and who cares, except a handful of long-faced people known as conservationists! Perhaps, after twirling our crystal ball we can gaze into the geologic future with Turgenef, whose vision was as clear as anyone else's:

Two huge masses, two giants rise aloft, one on each side of the horizon: the Jungfrau and the Finsteraarhorn. And the Jungfrau says to its neighbor: "What news hast thou to tell? Thou canst see better. What is going on there below?"

Several thousand years pass by like one minute. And the Finsteraarhorn rumbles in reply: "Dense clouds veil the earth . . . Wait!"

"Well, what now?" inquires the Jungfrau.

"Now I can see, down yonder, below; everything is still the same: party-colored, tiny. The waters gleam blue; the forests are black; heaps of stones piled up shine gray. Around them small beetles are still bustling—thou knowest, those two-legged beetles who have as yet been unable to defile either thou or me."

"Men?"

"Yes, men." Thousands of years pass, as it were one minute.

"Well, and what now?" asks the Jungfrau.

"I seem to see fewer of the little beetles. . . . Things have become clearer down below; the waters have contracted; the forests have grown thinner." More thousands of years pass, as it were one minute.

"What dost thou see?" says the Jungfrau.

"Things seem to have grown clearer round us, close at

hand . . . in the valleys there is still a spot, and something is moving."

"And now?" inquires the Jungfrau, after other thousands of years . . .

"Now it is well," replied the Finsteraarhorn, "everywhere is our snow, level snow and ice. Everything is congealed. It is well now, and calm."

"Good," said the Jungfrau. "But thou and I have chattered enough, old fellow. It is time to sleep."

"It is time!"

The huge mountains slumber; the green, clear heaven slumbers over the earth which has grown dumb forever.

PART TWO

"He was a friend to man, and lived in a house by the side of the road."—Homer

CHAPTER *8* ## SCHAUMBOCH'S: THE WAYSIDE TAVERN

There never was a house like Schaumboch's, the little stone house by the side of the mountain road. Its elevation at 1100 feet makes it the nearest house to heaven in all of the 920 square miles of Berks County. But its simple, quaint exterior and proximity to the abode of the blessed belie its iniquitous reputation. For Schaumboch's reputation is known, however vaguely, to old and young folks throughout the local Pennsylvania Dutch countryside.

If you should ask Grandma Hamm, of Eckville, or old Theo Fegley, of Drehersville, whether they would ever care to live up on the mountain, in the Schaumboch house, they would exclaim in horror, *"Ich wutt usht so leeb laeva mit em divel* (I would as soon live with the devil!)" Nor would any of the local old-timers be caught spending a single night in Schaumboch's. Once Ed Trexler, of Kempton, a solid, substantial Republican in his late seventies, enlivened a summer's evening for us with tales of the old house, which he knew so well as a boy. He also declared, with a furtive glance at the low ceiling, "I wouldn't sleep a night in this house if you paid me!"

My wife and I chuckle when folks like Ed Trexler allude to the ghosts that are reputed to infest the old house. Ours is perhaps the only house in the region in which ghosts have been well established. Many of the local people hold on to their Middle Age superstitions, and for several years we held on to the ghosts, enjoying their company.

Our introduction to Schaumboch's came in mid-September of 1934. At that time the property belonged to John E. Wenz, an elderly resident of Allentown. As we have explained in an earlier chapter, we were hospitably received by Mrs. Merkle, a kindly widow past middle age, and a friend of Mr. Wenz. She spent her summers in this isolated (and at the time) woefully run-down dwelling. Mrs. Merkle said not a word about any ghostly companions. Our sleeping quarters were in the attic, then roofed with nothing more than corrugated tin, peppered with holes. Well do we recall the stifling heat, the dingy little room scarcely ventilated by one small window, the wobbly bed which rocked like a dinghy, the cloudburst the first night which sent rain pelting athwart the bed, and, lastly, the inexplicable noises within the thick rock walls. Three nights were enough. We slipped down to Drehersville, three miles away.

"What!" croaked old Marberger, the village storekeeper, utter astonishment breaking out on his face when we told him we had slept "up there." He assured us that the ancient, dilapidated house on the mountain was haunted.

For nearly a hundred years the little house has been labeled *Schaumboch's*. There are a number of variants of the spelling. Our friend Minnie Ruppert, of Kempton, a former country schoolteacher, insists that the spelling should be Schwambach. Hadn't her parents known the old "cutthroat" and told her bristly tales about him when she was a girl? An old county map, published in 1876, indicates the site of the house on the east side of the mountain, as well as the name of its occupant: *Matthias Schambacher*. This is indeed the correct name. But we'll give way to present-day usage, for most of the local people remember the man as "Schaumboch."

The house was apparently built in Revolutionary times. Into its sinews went the most readily available materials: the hard, sandstone rock which forms the backbone of the Blue Mountain. It is low, solid, compact—a rectangular house with gable roof, built without benefit of a level. Its rock walls are eighteen inches thick. Many of the original beams, of hand-hewn oak, still support ceilings and floors. The whole structure is hopelessly out of plumb, and no two window frames are the same dimensions. Many old Pennsylvania Dutch houses have two identical front doorways, almost side by side, one leading into the living room, the other into the kitchen. The Schaumboch house has this interesting dual doorway. According to Henry K. Landis, foremost authority on Pennsylvania Dutch folkways, ". . . friendly calls were made at the kitchen door. The parlor was used for funerals, weddings, courting, and other formal occasions; it had the best furniture and cuspidors. There was no funny business about it, just practical housekeeping."

Just why anyone should want to build a house in such an isolated spot, high on the side of the mountain, has puzzled many of our friends. The mountain road, like many another ancient highway, was originally an Indian trail, and later a stagecoach highway providing a means of passage from the Great Valley to the sparsely settled regions to the West. The house was evidently a tavern from earliest times. Here horses and travelers could rest and quench their thirst at the only spring before resuming their way up the mountain pass. The old road also served a widespread charcoal industry. In Colonial times much of the local forest covering was converted into charcoal and carted to near-by Windsor Furnace, which was built around 1740. Here, during frontier days, stood a forge, a sawmill and a gristmill; crumbled masonry and a marker identify the site of the furnace. Dotting the Blue Mountain, and especially the Sanctuary, are peculiar flat areas, the charcoal burns, which kept the Furnace busy and which, in turn, helped to keep George Washington's armies supplied with weapons and cannon balls.

The earliest owner of the house of whom we have record was Jacob Gerhardt. He and his family lived here in 1793. Jacob, when a child of seven, survived one of the Indian atrocities that occurred locally in 1755-56. According to our friend, William H. Schroeder, of Kempton, whose knowledge of local history is unequaled, the Gerhardt cabin, alongside of the road at the foot of the mountain, was surrounded by Indians one February evening in 1756. The Indians called Jacob's father from the house, murdered him, and then set fire to the house, in which perished Jacob's mother, another woman, and five brothers and sisters. Only Jacob escaped; he had been concealed in some near-by bushes. (Local historical works present the details of this tragedy in substantially the same form.)

Little is known of Jacob Gerhardt and his family, except that they held title to the property for fifty-eight years. The property then passed into the hands of George and Priscilla Bolich (of a clan abundantly represented in Berks County), who owned the house for fifty-two years—and never lived in it, so far as we know. About the time that the Bolichs acquired the property, in 1851, Matthias Schambacher and his wife, Becky, appeared on the scene, having come from Philadelphia.

Many are the stories that are told of Schaumboch, as we shall now call him. He was described as of medium stature, lean but unusually strong; and as definitely the silent type of scoundrel. His grim character and reputation were said to be such that when little children saw him approaching in the valley, with horse and cart, they would run in terror. Becky Schaumboch, however, presented a wholesome contrast to her husband. She was slight, sweet-tempered, and well liked by all who knew her. It is certain that during the many years of their tenancy, the couple kept their mountain roost as a wayside inn.

Hucksters and farmers crossed the mountain frequently in those days; they sold their produce or merchandise in Orwigsburg, then the seat of Schuylkill County, or in Pottsville, which was growing rapidly and afforded good markets. Schaumboch's was a convenient place to rest weary horses. The wayfarer bought tobacco or candy, luncheon or liquor. There were also the men who quarried the pure sand at the very top of the mountain, to whom the Schaumbochs catered. And there were the teamsters who carried only coal from the near-by anthracite mines. All in all, the Schaumbochs did not want for trade.

An elderly mason from Auburn related this story to me when he came to do some work for us, late in 1939. He pointed to an open area across the road from the house. On that site, he said, once stood a small barn. One summer evening, a storm threatening, his father pulled up at Schaumboch's with a horse and team. He had hoped to stay overnight, if possible. Schaumboch told him to put the horse in the barn. But when he tried to do so, the animal reared up, neighed piteously and absolutely refused to enter the barn; possessed with terror, the horse acted as though it had seen a ghost. Entering the barn, the man found traces of fresh blood, whether of chicken, or steer, or whether human blood we are left to surmise. Anyway, with more trust in the wisdom of his horse than in Schaumboch's proffered hospitality, he departed in haste, despite the approaching storm. Other folks, laying great stress on the complex instinct of horses to sense something wrong, have told us how these animals usually shied away from Schaumboch's barn.

Another tale is related by Oscar Lutz, a jolly, robust character of seventy-eight years, who remembers Schaumboch as "a mean-looking man." Lutz, who lives in Kempton, told me the experience of a friend of his, Elias Featherolf, who has been dead these many years. Featherolf crossed the mountain on foot one summer's day when he was a young man. Passing Schaumboch's barn, he heard low moans and groans, and he went in to investigate. He found Schaumboch, hatchet in hand, in the loft of the barn. The sudden intrusion threw Schaumboch into paroxysms of fury. With menacing gestures, he shouted to Featherolf, "Go away; go away quick or I'll sink this hatchet in your head!" Featherolf gazed at the hatchet, then at Schaumboch's purple, malevolent countenance, and he took off like a frightened rabbit.

Ed Trexler relates the tale told him by his parents of a peddler passing through the Great Valley shortly after the Civil War, with a team laden with used uniforms and other garments. Usually such peddlers passed over the mountain, to be seen or heard from again in the Schuylkill Valley. This particular vendor was never seen again. But not so were his uniforms, for the elder Trexlers and their neighbors were amazed, months later, to see Schaumboch offering for sale the same clothing. Schaumboch also sold guns that had been used in the Civil War, according to Dan Bailey, of Eckville. Dan, who is eighty-five and remarkably alive, knew both Schaumbochs well. When I pressed him with questions, his gray, penetrating eyes flashed as memories crowded in upon him. His face beamed, and his voice shook with a torrent of words—wholly in German!

Dan and other folks will tell you that Schaumboch's method was the age-old dodge of coaxing prosperous-looking drummers into his barn for a drink. The unwary guest was treated to plenty of strong drink; and the rest was simple. Schaumboch is alleged to have killed eleven men, mostly drummers. We have been unable to find any remains of the hapless victims, though we have done plenty of searching!

It is amazing that the law never caught up with the much-feared miscreant. But then, in Schaumboch's time, the Blue Mountain was indeed wild and remote, the country roads were very rough, and the sheriff's office was many miles away. And as Joe Bailey, our nearest neighbor, has said, "Schaumboch was slippery."

One of Schaumboch's victims, it is believed, was an herb doctor named George Saylor, who was much respected among the people of Albany township. When Schaumboch was suspected of having killed Saylor, the local gentry decided that they had had enough of the evil inn-keeper. A petition was circulated throughout the valley—and there were many signers—to destroy the mountain tavern. William Schroeder, who told me the story, says that dynamite was obtained, all preparations were made and a date was set to blow up the house. At the eleventh hour, however, the local squire dissuaded the petitioners from carrying out their plan. So the house was spared, for which devotees of the Sanctuary will be ever grateful, but the rogue Schaumboch lived a few more years in unrepentant crime.

Schaumboch's last years found him full of infirmities and suffering a mental breakdown; possibly from long uneasiness with his conscience. He practically lived in a swivel-chair, from which he could scarcely move, according to Dan Bailey. Schaumboch's disordered mind made him say things, in the presence of visitors, which confirmed their suspicions of his early crimes. At length his wife, Becky, refused to allow anyone to see the old man; his confused talk was too self-damning! In 1879, at the age of fifty-five, Schaumboch went to his rest. He was buried in the cemetery of the New Bethel church, a few miles from Eckville, where we find his small gravemarker, with the incontrovertible designation: *Matthias Schambacher.*

Becky stayed on in the old house, with a niece from Port

Clinton for companionship. After her husband's death, the elderly *Frauen* of the countryside came often on Sundays to visit Becky. They were fond of the spirited, pink-cheeked old lady. They must have admired her courage and stamina, for it surely required those qualities, and more, for an aged woman to pull through the long winters on the mountain. Winters meant isolation, and continual effort to keep warm and comfortable. Eventually, around the turn of the century, Becky and her niece left the mountain to live with her brother in Port Clinton. This brother, named Mordas, was believed to have been an accomplice to some of the Schaumboch plundering. And there the thread of Schaumboch history ends, after a half century. Long before Becky's departure, the legend of the ghosts became well established; even Dan Bailey cannot recall when or how. But we shall tell of these ghosts, as *we* know them, in another chapter.

Before we take leave of Matthias Schaumboch, let us tell of another character of the Blue Mountain: Matthias Berger, whose personality was the antithesis of Schaumboch's. Though Berger was Schaumboch's nearest neighbor, it is unlikely that the two men saw much of each other, for Berger was a recluse, whose humble dwelling was situated well off in the woods, far from the road and about a mile south of the tavern. I have met only three persons who knew the old hermit, and one of these is Dan Bailey. As a boy, Dan often hiked up into the mountains to visit with the kindly, pious Berger, who lived alone in his "shanty" (as Dan called it) for twenty-eight years. When he needed money, Matthias Berger trudged down to the valley and offered his services to the farmers. He was a good worker and in demand, but like the famous recluse of Walden Pond, Berger worked only when he had to. One day, about sixty years ago, he was found brutally murdered a few yards from his shanty, which had been badly torn up, as though the devil himself had pillaged. Berger's body was discovered by Michael Hendricks, the grandfather of our friend Schroeder. The stone foundation of a little house, near a lovely fern-hung spring, deep in the shadows of the mountain and just off the southern edge of the Sanctuary, is all that reminds us of Matthias Berger, the hermit.

For two decades following the Schaumboch epoch, the house was occupied by William Turner, his wife, and their eight children. How the ten Turners managed to turn round in their tiny domicile, without trampling on one another, was a question that bothered us, until one wild week end in 1942 when sixteen house guests descended on us.

The Turners kept up the tradition of tavern-keeping. William Turner was a man of considerable bulk—three hundred pounds—we have been told. He was never very well or able to move about easily. His sedentary days were spent behind a thirteen-foot counter or bar (a section of which we have preserved), serving beer, Blue Mountain tea, schnapps and sandwiches to the woodsmen and farmers whose business led them over the mountain. In the fall many of his customers were the hawk-shooters who swarmed over the mountain. Many a passer-by has told us wistfully about drinking Blue Mountain tea at Turner's in "the good old days." This tea was made of the anise-scented leaves of the sweet goldenrod *(Solidago suaveolens);* sometimes it was combined with applejack to produce an "out of this world" effect.

Education for the eight Turner children must have been a difficult matter, especially in the winter months, when treacherous ice or deep snow mantled the steep, rough road. The young Turners had to trudge three miles to the one-room grade school in Eckville. Some of the Turner progeny may still be found living within twenty miles.

In the early spring of 1922, the Turners abandoned the

rugged mountain life. The property, consisting of the house and three acres of orchards, was sold for seven hundred dollars to John E. Wenz, mentioned earlier in our chronicle. Schaumboch's was now in for another colorful phase in its history. Wenz spent week ends during summers and hunting seasons, entertaining a bunch of cronies. In the early days of the Sanctuary, it took us an entire season to clean up the broken beer and whiskey bottles, the heaps of clam shells and other debris.

During these years Schaumboch's is described as nothing more than a camp, a rendezvous for roisterers—until the Prohibition Era. And then the real fun began! Wenz rented his property to a gang of bootleggers, the leader a resident of near-by Orwigsburg. The bootleggers soon had a cozy, efficient gin plant in operation, in the dungeon-like cellar of the house. And though the house was guarded vigilantly night and day, curiously enough it was not lived in. The gin-makers camped in the little shed near the house, built originally by the Turners to house chickens. It has since been remodeled and has provided overnight shelter during the fall for visitors to the Sanctuary, including several illustrious ornithologists.

About 1930, Schaumboch's aroused the suspicions of Federal prohibition agents. One cold fall morning two agents attempted to enter Schaumboch's and the chicken shed. From the latter came threats and warnings that it was an unhealthy place for strangers. But the agents were a determined pair. Suddenly a pistol shot spluttered from the shed. The two agents took cover and returned the shots. To their amazement, two young women dashed from the shed, in bare feet and thin dresses, and fled into the woods. More exchange of shots. Then one of the agents departed, leaving the other to keep the place covered. But it was not long before he returned, from Reading apparently, with some forty defenders of the law, who swarmed over the place like gulls attracted to a garbage-dump. They literally shot and crashed their way into the house, and the two bootleggers gave in before such overwhelming opposition. The law-enforcement officers found one of the biggest stills that they had ever seized in this region. And before they were through they turned Wenz's rendezvous into wreckage. Poor Wenz! I can still hear him groan when he told me how costly it had been to repair ceilings and walls and to replace furnishings.

Even so, Schaumboch's for several years remained a pathetic sight, having degenerated to a forlorn hovel by the time my wife and I came along. A few thirsty travelers continued to drop in, even after Schaumboch's became Sanctuary property. One day in the fall of 1939 a huge man filled our doorway, and filled us with wondering when he asked, "Can I buy a drink?" A moment of perplexed silence, and he inquired further, "Don't you sell no schnapps?" My wife called out from across the kitchen table, "There's a good spring across the road, if you are thirsty!"

However dilapidated, ever since the Sanctuary's beginning we had coveted Schaumboch's, its three acres of old orchard and the unfailing spring, all of which adjoined the Sanctuary property on the east. Historic Schaumboch's, once it could be treated to the needed repairs and improvements, would prove ideal as the Sanctuary headquarters. For three years Wenz refused to consider any proposals for its purchase. In the summer of 1938, however, he had a sudden change of mind.

Schaumboch's became the property of the Hawk Mountain Sanctuary Association through the generosity of Mrs. Raymond V. Ingersoll, one of the directors of the Association. Wenz parted with his domain for the sum of $1052.50. Nobody else would give him half that amount, but he held out on his price, and not a cent less. I never understood what the fifty cents was for.

And so we arrived, my wife and I and Dukie, our cocker spaniel, on August 30th, ready to move in. The place was an unholy mess, and the little house was hopelessly cluttered with worn-out furnishings. Wenz came along and urged us to buy all the furnishings. Heaven forbid! Having nothing ourselves, we could have used, temporarily, the kitchen range (a good one), an oil heater, two or three chairs and the kitchen table; possibly a bed, of which there were four in the house. Wenz was slightly wobbly, with a gallon of apple-jack in tow which he offered to us, with urging to "drink hearty." But he was not exactly in a mellow mood. "You must take it all or nothing," Wenz said. We offered to buy only what we could use. But it was "all or nothing," and we decided on nothing. Then Wenz left, greatly exercised because we were uncharitably disposed toward his household effects. Before we knew it, he was back with a truck and driver and, with more energy than we thought the old codger capable of, the house was stripped to a pin.

We sat up housekeeping in Schaumboch's with nothing more than a gasoline cookstove, some candles, and a rickety bench salvaged from the rubble outdoors. Our good friends, the Reverend Edward S. Frey and his lovely wife, Maria, of Lemoyne, appeared about this time. They were wonderful sports. They camped with us for four days and pitched in to help lighten our load. On the second day, Maria helped my wife to scrub the floors, which looked as though they had never seen a mop. I carried bucket after bucket of water from the spring across the road; the girls promptly dashed the clear water across the floors, upon the walls, wading ankle deep, singing and laughing, and wielding their mops with energy born of great satisfaction. Thus on the eve of its new era, Schaumboch's was appropriately baptized! In due time, the house began to sparkle with cleanliness and a few essential furnishings which we purchased in Reading. Cleaning up the house and grounds proved a tremendous undertaking, but it had its entertaining aspects. In the evening, the tired girls warmed up water and took their baths in the kitchen. But it was my custom to jump into the icy spring. On an occasion such as this, while I was scrubbing off the day's grime, I heard a car laboring up the rough, dirt road. Seizing a large bath towel which was all I had for covering, I scrambled up into the woods. Peering from behind a tangle of rhododendron to see who had disturbed my bath, I discovered that I had already been discovered by Mrs. Edge. The woods rang with laughter. We slept outdoors for about a fortnight, using camp cots, and sleeping bags. Before dawn we were awakened by the deer "snorting" in the orchard, and by a whippoorwill calling close by.

A beautiful slate roof replaced the tin roof so full of holes. This was accomplished in the waning of 1938, our former patron again coming to the rescue. The roof was an amusing drama in itself; amusing, that is, from the perspective of a few years.

In mid-December of 1938, a gang of carpenters arrived from Hamburg, under contract to re-roof the house in fourteen calendar days. A dubious contract, if there ever was one. For the time being, the road was clear. But only two weeks earlier twelve and a half inches of snow, the gift of a Thanksgiving day blizzard, made our road completely impassable. Thanks to the intervention of mild weather and three days of rain which melted all the snow, the men were able to start work on December 13th. That day most of the roof came off. The uncovered debris included a desiccated cave rat. Two days later we had half a roof over our heads. That night the temperature dipped to 12°; we saw Orion, neatly framed between the new rafters and the gaping half roof. In the morning the temperature was 15°—much too cold for the carpenters to work, so they huddled in the kitchen with us until the morning sun warmed up their project. While the carpenters moved briskly on the job, I kept warm collecting and burning an enormous amount of trash, much of which had been stored in the walls by genera- tions of rodents. On December 21st: snow flurries all day; and the unfinished job made us jittery, but the weatherman was cooperative, holding in abeyance any snowstorms. Two days later the slaters were completing the job. Bleak skies and the prospect of snow made the men work furiously. A driving snow squall at noonday kept the men on the job, not one stopping to eat lunch! The roofing job was finished that day. Christmas Eve brought sub-freezing weather, sleet and slippery roads. But Schaumboch's was safe. The next day found us on Cape Cod, where we were able to enjoy a well-earned holiday.

The little stone house by the side of the road has served admirably as Sanctuary headquarters. In a sense it has reached the ultimate refinement of its early career as a tav- ern. For under our roof in recent years have slept mission- aries and geologists, professors and writers, and just workaday folks—a gathering that would have made old Schaumboch blink with wonder. Certainly we have poured tea and coffee enough to have drowned all the former occupants of the house.

Little by little we have remodeled and renovated, pulled down and built up, from cellar to roof, at much expense and huge, unending toil. Usually our only opportunity of im- proving the place has been during the busy fall months when hawks and human visitors converged on the Sanctuary to take up the major part of our time and energies. In that first pioneering fall some simple plumbing was installed. Running water in an honest-to-goodness kitchen sink and a flush toilet on the second floor were improvements which Schaumboch's could boast of for the first time in one hundred fifty years.

Everything went well with the old house until the war years. Then for three long years it was unoccupied. When my wife and I finally returned, in March of 1946, Schaumboch's had a haunted, hopeless, down-in-the-heel look. To save the place, a tremendous overhauling was needed at once. I turned carpenter, plasterer, mason and painter; Mrs. Broun turned painter, paper-hanger and general factotum. Materials were hard to obtain, but lumber, wallboard, cement and a score of other items eventually found their way. So did Scott Dearolf, long a stanch and loyal friend of the Sanctuary. Scott spent most of the spring with us, laboring long and arduous hours, becoming adept at using creosote and mixing concrete. It was slow work and often exhausting. But Schaumboch's was restored during that eventful spring. Among other improvements was a new cement cellar, tidy and waterproof, in which we dug two feet or more without uncovering any of the bones of sinister old Schaumboch's murdered victims!

One day in July, 1947, I met Sam Greenawalt down in Kempton, a big, jovial, kindly-looking man who had come home from upstate New York with his family to enjoy a brief holiday. He hailed me with a smile. "You are Maurice Broun, aren't you? I know all about you!" I had never seen the man before, and I was nonplused. Then he told me how, as a State Trooper in 1941, he was assigned the job of investigating the Sanctuary, and the occupants of Schaumboch's in particular, as a potential nest of Nazis. War was pending, and people were hysterical. It was all deadly serious then. Now Greenawalt laughed loudly. But when I pressed him for details, his only reply was that the whole story was "confidential" and locked away in the files of the State Police in Harrisburg. Thus Schaumboch's once more had achieved official notoriety.

Long before meeting Sam Greenawalt, however, I had pieced together much of the story of how we were watched and suspected of being Nazis. It began in one of the local barrooms, logically enough, for where else could loose and idle talk so easily generate? A group of hunters, grousing about the Sanctuary because no hunting was permitted within the area, were speculating over their beer as to the purpose and intent of all the crowds that gathered upon the mountain. Why were all those people camping around Schaumboch's each week end during the fall? One fellow, who evidently had had too many beers, reported that he had seen a huge dog guarding Schaumboch's, and that the dog was in the custody of a man in uniform, carrying a rifle. Another character insisted that up in the woods, beyond the house, there was a big ammunition dump. Someone else said he saw someone signaling from one of the lookouts on the mountain. (The person sending the supposed signals was Professor F. J. Trembley wielding a butterfly net!) Since so many of the strange people came in cars with out-of-state license plates, they must be Nazis! Why, of course they're a bunch of Nazis up there! This sensational conclusion was bandied about by more barroom frequenters until at length it came to the ears of the State Police. Enter Sam Greenawalt and other State Troopers.

At the time of the investigation, in the summer of 1941, Professor Trembley and his wife, Isabel, spent three weeks in Schaumboch's. They were watched continuously. As the Trembleys relaxed on the back porch, they saw an aeroplane come in low over the Eck. Not once, but many times it circled in wide sweeps over the Sanctuary woods, in search of the ammunition dump, perhaps. The lack of traffic, the dead quiet of the mountain in summer when bird lovers and Sanctuary enthusiasts were absent, must have baffled the investigators. They went down to Mrs. Koch's home, in Drehersville, to examine her register of scores of week end guests of the Sanctuary. They studied and checked up on many of the names, some of them Jewish, they remarked with surprise to Mrs. Koch. They had the F. B. I. look up Mrs. Edge and all the directors of the Sanctuary, including the Brouns. They returned to the mountain and snooped around Schaumboch's, from the woods. They found no huge dogs, no uniforms, nor arms nor ammunition caches; only a harmless biologist and his wife, from Bethlehem, taking life easy.

So we close our chapter on Schaumboch's. But tradition and history will continue to be made in the little stone house by the side of the road; for there never was a house like Schaumboch's! Even the United States Post Office is aware of that, for occasionally we receive letters delivered promptly, addressed to:

> Schaumboch's
> Hawk Mountain Sanctuary,
> Pennsylvania.

THE GHOSTS
OF SCHAUMBOCH'S:

CHAPTER 9

Adventures with Wood Rats

Pigs is pigs, and rats is rats—that is, if you don't know your rats! This is the story of an animal that is well worth knowing, a rat that is gentle and friendly, not at all destructive and, what is more, a complete American. Let me introduce the *Alleghany wood rat,* also known as cave rat, a squirrel-like creature that was little known scientifically until 1893. Have you ever seen a cave rat? You've not even heard of the thing, probably, for cave rats are local, restricted to a particular habitat and, like bats and other eerie creatures, they bestir themselves largely at night.

Peter Kalm, the natural historian, in his celebrated *Travels* published in 1771, says, "Mr. Bartram maintained that before Europeans settled here rats had been in the country, for he saw a great many of them in the high mountains which are commonly called the Blue Mountains, where they lived among stones and in the subterraneous grottos which are in those mountains. They always lie very close in the daytime, and you hardly ever see one out; but at night they come out, and make a terrible noise." A terrible noise, indeed!

John Bartram, the roving, versatile naturalist, evidently became familiar with the wood rat in the fall of 1736, during a trip up the Schuylkill River, into and beyond the "Blue

Mountains"—our Kittatinny Ridge. The Kittatinny, with its extensive rock slides and "subterraneous grottos," has been the home of our wood, or cave rat, since time immemorial. Hawk Mountain (a spur of the Blue Mountains) is in the same general area that was visited by Bartram.

When my wife and I arrived at the Schaumboch house in the late summer of 1938, soon after it had been acquired by the Hawk Mountain Sanctuary Association, the house had not been occupied for months. The first few nights of our occupancy, Schaumboch's ghosts celebrated the occasion in high spirits. Shortly after dusk, we heard dull thumping sounds across the attic floors, and there were strange bangings and rattlings, like the clattering of utensils that might have belonged to some long-since-liquidated hardware drummer. Sudden crashes resounded on the cellar stairs. Then all would be quiet again. That is, reasonably quiet, for our young cocker spaniel went into tail spins of excitement with all these obstreperous manifestations of the occult. In the wee hours of the morning, Bartram's "terrible noises" took place spasmodically.

I suppose some ghosts are reserved and gentle, but Schaumboch's ghosts seemed to be possessed of the devil. But what the devil were these devils? We were going to find out, in the forthright manner that Dan Webster handled his devil. So, on a gloomy morning in September, I ripped open a ceiling of one of the rooms, and down crashed the strangest debris that ever we did see. First we gathered up a bushel basket full of what had been a nest—a mass of dried grasses and leaves, twigs, fungi, wood chips, scraps of paper, desiccated apples; and then we swept up a pailful of acorns and weed fragments. Next we descended into the darkness of the windowless cellar measuring twenty-four by thirty feet. Our spotlight illuminated another pile of debris, and two neat nests with openings on their sides, reminding us of the nests of ovenbirds, on a grand scale. A pilot blacksnake, considerably more than six feet long, poured itself like a stream of ink out of a dark corner, slithered across the dirt floor, almost under our noses, and disappeared into a low crack in the damp wall. Continuing our search, we saw a rat slink furtively along the wall; it paused momentarily and its eyes were fixed in the glare of the light. It was a rather innocent-appearing creature, with large thin ears, and great black eyes that looked up at us appealingly; its tail was long and hairy, its upperparts grayish-brown, and its feet and underparts white. Its whole appearance suggested a Gargantuan deer mouse. Could this innocuous-looking creature be the cause of nocturnal pandemonium? It could!

So I had met up with a cave rat, an animal which we New Englanders had never seen. But this was not a conventional cave rat, whose home should have been out in the woods, beneath some rock pile. This was a sophisticated rat, with two homes in our cellar which made a great cozy cave, whose four walls and superstructure provided labyrinthine passages in which to lurk and lay up great stocks of fortunately not too smelly food. Here was the devil—or one of them—withal a modest, puny one, cornered in his den. Brother Rat was not expunged, but the cellar was ruthlessly cleared of all his works. Most of the larger holes in the cellar walls were plugged up. That night Schaumboch's ghosts were still in evidence, but their spirits were low, apparently, for the weird noises were few and faint.

A full year passed, during most of which we were absent from the old house. But promptly on our return we were attracted to Schaumboch's cellar, as a bat is drawn to a belfry.

A huge pile of the usual debris: dried weeds, grasses, twigs, mushrooms, and papers, and a sizable rat's nest confronted us. But the harvester was not at home. We were intrigued by a number of neatly stacked bundles of mints and other

Maurice Broun at Pleasant Valley Sanctuary, Lenox, Massachusetts.

The sad harvest of "sport": 230 dead hawks picked up at one spot near the Lookout in October 1932.

A red-tailed hawk, hung from the Drehersville bridge to taunt the Brouns, served instead to help the Sanctuary obtain funds.

Rosalie Edge, founder of Hawk Mountain Sanctuary.

Irma Broun, The Keeper of the Gate, in 1935, when the Sanctuary was operated by the Emergency Conservation Committee of New York.

The North Lookout, elevation 1521 feet, from which the famous fall flights of hawks were first observed.

View north from the Sanctuary's Lookout.

Another Lookout view to the north.

Maurice Broun on
the Lookout.

"A Sunday in mid-October 1936—750 visitors registered, and plenty of hawks."
—M. Broun

Schaumboch's, looking dreary and run-down, when it was acquired by the Sanctuary in 1938.

Schaumboch's renovated. In those days, its elevation at 1100 feet made it the nearest house to heaven in Berks County.

Maurice and Irma Broun's wedding photo, January 15, 1934.

Rare casual photo of Maurice and Irma with cocker spaniel puppies.

Maurice entitled this "The monk in Schaumboch's cell," taken in January 1939.

Snapshot from a family album, inside a renovated Schaumboch's.

Eastern evening grosbeaks at the feeder outside Schaumboch's window.

Schaumboch's ghost discovered. A wood rat and nest debris.

Irma and Maurice saw wood.

Irma milks one of the goats.

Irma Broun (left) selling Emergency Conservation Committee pamphlets at the trail entrance, September 1937.

Teaching school and scout groups behind Schaumboch's cottage.

Maurice Broun holds his 18-power binoculars.

Rosalie Edge and red-tailed hawk, early 1940s.

Maurice Broun and Roger Tory Peterson, 1941.

Roger Tory Peterson, in his sleeping bag under Schaumboch's porch, 1955.

Willard Van Name (fourth from right), curator at the American Museum of Natural History and member of the Emergency Conservation Committee, gave the initial $500 to Edge for lease of the Mountain.

Rachel Carson on North Lookout, October, 1946.

Maurice at North Lookout, September 30, 1959, and, below, photographing young long-eared owls, two years before he retired as curator. Today his photographs represent a documentary account of the Sanctuary's history.

"Red-tail coming over No. 4" says a voice on the telephone, as the author scans the far ridge for the oncoming bird and prepares to time its speed-of-flight.

Views from the Lookout, winter 1939.

In the Ice King's grip.

The Brouns on Strawberry Hill Farm, 1978.

weeds, perhaps the fare for Sundays and special occasions. This time I disturbed nothing.

That evening I descended again into the cellar. The opening of the big nest was filled with the face of a cave rat. Leisurely, the creature stepped forth and retired to a corner. It was sleek and handsome, in perfect "form" and positively enormous. The books on mammals give the average length of the Alleghany wood rat as seventeen and a half inches from tip of nose to tip of tail. This animal easily measured twenty inches, and it was docile as it was ample. Upstairs we held a council to determine the fate of the rat: to be or not to be, that was the question. We decided that it would be interesting to permit the rat to remain and to learn something about it; so the animal carried on, enjoying life, liberty and the pursuit of happiness.

Throughout the autumn we proudly exhibited our burly specimen to many an inquisitive guest, scarcely any of whom had ever seen a live cave rat. The rat took all the publicity very well; it took us for granted, and didn't budge from its quarters, even when I went to get a hod of coal. Meanwhile. its stores of winter provender became more voluminous, threatening to take up the whole of the cellar floor. The most surprising thing about our friend, however, was its quietness. We heard the rat every night, to be sure, but we were only agreeably aware of its presence, like a good friend shuffling around the house. Even Duke, our cocker spaniel, grew tolerant of the rat. A single hole in the base of the stone wall at the foot of the cellar stairway provided the rat's only means of getting outdoors. As a matter of record, I must state that (rarely) I encountered two mature cave rats in the cellar.

Winter came on and we had decided to hibernate at Schaumboch's. For seven long weeks we were snowed in, out of contact with the world except for the radio, but we were one happy family—my wife and I, Duke, and Mother Rat, for by now we had determined her sex. Though she had ample stores of natural food, we "babied" her along with frequent tidbits of bread, apples, carrots and other edibles, all of which she accepted. Nor was Mother Rat all alone in her lair; twice during the winter a big brown bat snapped out of its hibernating torpor to whisk around the cellar, having evidently entered through the cellar door sometime during the fall. And there were countless hundreds of "cave crickets" of all sizes swarming over the walls, which also afforded a happy hunting ground for several very fat spiders. In spite of much snow, we knew that Mother Rat took an airing each night, for we never found her excrement in the cellar, and her tracks in the snow were numerous. Our winter of solitude on the mountain passed most pleasantly. In April we closed Schaumboch's for several months.

Returning the succeeding September, we found Mother Rat still snugly ensconced in the cellar—with a family. Three half-grown young filled the bulky home. But the old lady had become noticeably timid; she resented our prying. The young rats would scamper out of sight at our approach. They were singularly quiet and continued to live with their mother for several weeks, becoming more and more aloof, until one day they disappeared, perhaps having been driven off by the old lady, as a mother robin might drive her young into new territory.

Our relations with Mother Rat continued friendly, and not too eventful, through three years. We were dismayed at times to find the cellar overflowing with her foodstuffs, which made Heinz' 57 varieties look picayune. Some of the accumulation had to be cleared out periodically. Although her province was the cellar, now and then she ventured on a trip into the attic walls. Then we would hear noises which reminded us of our early experiences.

Our periodic absences continued. Finding Mother Rat still "at home" in September, 1942, was like a warm and cheering welcome. But the cloudbursts over eastern Pennsylvania the previous June had badly gullied the mountain road, making it impassable for weeks. We could imagine how wet her abode had been all summer, for we found the inside of Schaumboch's heavily encrusted with mildew, and we were obliged to camp out for nearly two weeks. Under these conditions we began to view with increasing irritation and intolerance the immense amount of sticks and leaves and trash of all kinds that the old lady kept bringing in.

On a certain fateful day in October, I said, "Enough is enough. We can't have the whole woods brought in to the cellar." But to remove the gentle furry friend of four years' standing was almost unthinkable. Then I toyed with an idea. Why not find out how much homing instinct the old girl had. If she returned from an appreciable distance, she would find her home spick and span, ready for a new lease, and she would be welcome as usual to live with us. Trapping her in a humane box-trap was easily accomplished. Mother Rat and I then journeyed to the Lookout atop the mountain, a mile from Schaumboch's. There I released my charge, and, with some bewilderment, she soon disappeared among the great loose rocks. I must confess that I felt mean and small for what I had done. But the Lookout must have its good points, for cave rats frolic there the year round—and Mother Rat never returned.

Schaumboch's ghosts came to life again that very night. The goings-on in the cellar, in the old walls, over the kitchen ceiling, were simply incredible. Most of the night was filled with Bartram's "terrible noises." The next evening the humane trap was set in the cellar; the night passed with relative quiet, and in the morning a sizable ghost squatted complacently in the trap, munching an apple. And thus I toted another cave rat to the Lookout, noting carefully its markings, and any physical peculiarities.

Almost nightly now, for ten nights, Schaumboch's walls resounded with sounds scarcely to be described, except possibly by a demonologist. Reviewing the extraordinary history of the place, from the time a half century ago when a religious recluse, Matthias Berger, was murdered in cold blood in his little retreat on our mountain, to Schaumboch's legendary multiple-murders, and the enormous still which prohibition agents found when they raided the house in the dry era, it seemed as though all the evils of the past were being translated into mad and monstrous sounds.

And as fast as the ghosts were captured and transported to the Lookout, other ghosts took over. Six ghosts in all, no two alike in size or markings, were carried off the premises. Apparently the woods were filled with ghosts, which, once exorcised, were gone forever. But we sighed for the good old days of peace with Mother Rat. Now we began to appreciate her, and to understand her important function in maintaining order among ghosts.

The seventh cave rat which we trapped commanded our special attention. She was only slightly smaller than Mother Rat. But she looked like a tough customer, as though she had survived the Battle of Dunkirk. Her right ear had a deep and ugly rip, making the ear appear cleft; a lower lip showed a raw and severe wound; and there was a chunk missing from her tail. Old Cleft-ear, as I called her, had a wicked, aggressive gleam in her eyes.

"An old battle-ax," I thought to myself, "and just the girl we need. You're hired!" Returning to the cellar, I lowered the trap gently and released the rat. Evidently Cleft-ear took me seriously, for she lumbered off as calmly as you please, like an imperturbable veteran. Nor did she go very far. A few minutes later I returned to the cellar and found her looking over the old nests. She stayed.

Tranquillity had returned with Cleft-ear. She did a smart job of keeping out all clamorous and clangorous competitors. "Good girl," we would say to her when we deposited dainty morsels by her domicile. And we learned a lesson—that when you monkey with nature, you're inviting a plague of—shall we say rats!

Returning to Schaumboch's after the war, one of the first things we did was to lay a cement floor in the cellar. This and other improvements discouraged the cave rats from entering the house. In the spring of 1948, I found one of our old friends in a bird banding trap. She was an enormous rat and round as a canteloupe, from too much good living on bird seed; she was blind in the right eye and her right ear was cleft! When released she lumbered into the rock wall by our back porch, where she continues to dwell as this is written.

CHAPTER *10* ### ALL SORTS OF PEOPLE

One day in the summer of 1946 my wife answered a knock at Schaumboch's door, and in over the threshold popped an inquisitive stranger with this pretty little speech: "I'm just a nosy old woman, but I'd like to come in to see your house. I used to come by here in a wagon, with my father, when I was a child." And without further ado, the woman satisfied her curiosity with a hasty examination of the old beams of the kitchen ceiling, our simple domestic arrangements, ourselves—and she was off. Through the years of our life on Hawk Mountain, this experience has been repeated scores of times, with variations, of course. But this particular nosybody (if we may be permitted to coin a word) was at least a lady; she *did* knock! Many strangers, including graduate students of the better colleges, have walked into Schaumboch's without knocking.

I suppose one reason why we have never become bored with Hawk Mountain is the unpredictable, spicy human element which flavors the job. This is not to imply, however, that we take interruptions like sweet-tempered angels. Oh, no! Time and again, behind closed doors, we have let off steam! Though they may take heavy toll of our time and energy, routine interruptions are a part of the game, and so we have come to regard most of them with amusement or good-humored resignation. It is the price anyone must pay who would choose to live in a public place. And as public places go, Hawk Mountain is indeed a natural. . . .

In the early years of the Sanctuary the execrable mountain road was so hard on automobiles that rarely did anyone venture up, except honest-to-goodness bird watchers, who were willing to take their chances on cracked oil pans, broken axles, or mutilated tires. An improved dirt road in 1937 and an enormous amount of newspaper publicity brought more and more people, all sorts of people. The Sanctuary's accessibility now made the notorious Schaumboch's house an object of great curiosity—more so when it became a part of the Sanctuary and the home of the curator and his wife. Perhaps the majority of the people who nose their cars over the mountain for the first time do so out of sheer curiosity to see what it is all about. Some of these people linger awhile, enjoy the prospects, and get acquainted with us; we have made many fine friends even among the merely inquisitive. But the comings and goings of the well-known human race, in our seemingly remote wilderness, have been a continual source of wonderment to my wife and me. Conversely, many of our visitors must be tremendously curious about *us*, and our mode of living far up on the mountain, in a house of formerly discreditable character, with no neighbors, no telephone, no electricity, nor apparently any of the other amenities of so-called civilization. In any case, it seems to us that most of the people who cross the mountain for the first time are drawn to Schaumboch's with an irresistible impulse to knock on the door and have a look-see.

So life at Schaumboch's "by the side of the road" has its drawbacks. In the fall of the year especially, we may enjoy as much privacy as the proverbial goldfish. I remember one young woman—a perfect stranger—who walked in one late evening during the busy fall and, without a word, she took off her city shoes and stockings to change into hiking boots;

only after ten minutes or so did it occur to any of us to enter into the formalities of an introduction!

Many times people have stopped their cars by the house, walked onto the stoop as casually as though they were mounting the White House steps, and then peered into our windows, with noses pressed against the panes! More than once my wife has pulled the curtain on such rudeness. In the spring of 1947, hoping to gain some measure of privacy, we erected a stout rustic railing in front of the house. We were agreeably surprised to find that this simple device reduced the windowpane type of nosyness by about ninety per cent. But a more adroit form of curiosity-seeking developed. In spite of the very obvious spring, flowing free and pure opposite the house, people sometimes knock on the door to ask for a drink of water—actually to get a look at the hillbillies in their den.

One cold, blustery fall day, some ladies from Ohio, not too appropriately clad, were waiting in the road for other members of their party, and casting wistful glances in the direction of the house. They were shivering from the cold, apparently, so my wife invited them into the kitchen to warm up. But they were not interested in the friendly warmth of the stove. "We just wanted to get in to see the place," was their starkly candid confession.

There are many many knocks at the door (especially at mealtimes) which materialize into a question that we have answered *ad infinitum, ad nauseum:* "Where does this road go?" One summer day, feeling in especially good humor, I took pains to explain to a pleasant, elderly gentleman more than the basic fact that the road came up the mountain and that it most certainly went down the mountain. Then the man asked, "By the way, what's this Sanctuary all about?" Again I explained, while my wife waited impatiently for me to come to dinner. "Oh! wildlife is my hobby. This is a wonderful thing!" So Mr. Fegley signed up as a *Hawk Mountaineer*, with no coaching on my part. About a year and some five thousand people later, came the knock on the door, just as we sat down to lunch. "Don't you remember me?" inquired a septuagenarian who did indeed look familiar. We had had a busy morning, visitors had been on hand as early as 7 A.M., and I could not collect my wits. I replied, "Vaguely." Our visitor beamed and said, "Why, that's my name—Fegley—what a remarkable memory you have!" And after a really pleasant visit, Mr. Fegley pulled out four dollars to renew his membership for two years.

Then there were the well-groomed Chicagoans who had made a special trip to the Sanctuary. Irma and I had been working hard in our oldest, dirtiest clothes, cleaning soot from the kitchen stove; we must have presented a rough, wild appearance. The lady from the great city looked Irma over from toes to hair-do, slowly and methodically, as though she were regarding a human relic of prehistoric times. The travelers wanted to know where they could spend the night. So I directed them to the Koch's, in Drehersville, merely a matter of driving in a straight line for three and a half miles. But the pilot of the car, accustomed to pavements and city blocks apparently, was taking no chances in this God-forsaken backwoods. He drew out a compass and proceeded to get his bearings. . . .

Between Schaumboch's, the Sanctuary entrance, and the Lookout, we have seen the gamut of human society. It is as though all types have passed through the Needle's Eye, helping to create the colorful threads of Hawk Mountain history. Into our ken have come the affluent and the destitute, poets and pundits, men of every persuasion. I shall never forget the day, early in the Sanctuary's beginnings, when a millionaire from Philadelphia spent a few very pleasant and rewarding hours at the Lookout, with his two children. I wondered whether an angel might be hovering over the Sanctuary, which for years had been as impoverished as a church mouse. The angel fled, however, with the millionaire, who purchased a few pamphlets and left a thirty-five-cent donation to the Sanctuary.

A few days following the millionaire's visit, a curious character awaited me at the Lookout. I had finished making myself comfortable for a morning of bird-watching, when I heard the scraping of rocks behind me, and there, only a few paces from me, was an incredible figure, fresh from the pages of Dickens. The man was large and heavy, and his massive jaw, drooling tobacco juice, was covered with a week's growth of stubble; his clothing, from head to foot, consisted of unspeakably dirty rags. He was improvising a fireplace among the rocks. I hailed him, and he stood up, startled. The man proved to be a half-wit, with a feeble, almost incomprehensible way of talking, in Pennsylvania Dutch. I warned him against building a fire and he obediently put aside the sticks. There before him, spread on a flat rock, was a lot of crushed honeycomb and a wad of bright red paper. He was a bee-hunter and had just arrived, having tramped cross-country and up over the ridge, from New Ringgold, three miles to the north. Never having witnessed the procedure of going after a beehive with syrupbox and oil of anise, I decided to let him go about his purpose, and we became friendly. By noon more than a hundred bees had gathered to his boxes, while he was off scouting for the hive, which he did not locate. He was my only visitor that day, and certainly the oddest character I have ever encountered on the mountain. I never saw the man again.

Almost as strange as the tatterdemalion, but far less comprehensible, was the slight, gray-haired, wild-eyed man I once found along the road, dipping dirty water from one small puddle to another, using a couple of tin cans. I gazed down upon this absurd performance for a long time, scarcely believing my eyes and trying to figure out what manner of madness possessed the man. But he was enjoying his simple play with nature's most abundant element, and perhaps he wasn't too far removed from such simpletons as spend their time watching hawks! I did not disturb the puddle-maker.

I have had many pleasant and stimulating contacts with naturalists at our Lookout; and I have met all kinds of odd characters as well. I think the man who most surprised me, however, was a mild, really intelligent gentleman of seventy-six, from Philadelphia, who looked up into the deep blue at high noon, to behold, with utter astonishment—the moon! He said that in all his years this was the first time he had seen the moon in broad daylight. What a confession for an old man! Think of all the simple outdoor joys this man must have missed.

One quiet, sunny September day, I was alone at the Lookout, when there suddenly appeared close beside me a frail little lady, leaning on the arm of her chauffeur. She had shown considerable courage in climbing the trail, even rougher in those days before the war than it is today. She seated herself in a matter of fact way on a rock and we had a good talk together, as though in her sittingroom at home. We had a cup of milk from my thermos. She asked no searching questions but appeared to enjoy what I could tell her of the landscape spread to view. When rested, she said good-by and returned down the trail. A few days after, she wrote to Mrs. Edge, reporting her visit to the Sanctuary. "I was driving from Buckhill Falls to Philadephia," she said, "and stopped to see your Sanctuary. My purpose in going to Philadelphia was to make my will, and I write to tell you that I left a bequest to Hawk Mountain Sanctuary. Your curator has very good manners."

The questions that have been fired at me by inexperienced observers at the Lookout range from the sublime to the ridiculous. I think the prize question came from a lady from New Jersey who, after witnessing with us a red-tail flying just under the Lookout, with a mouse in its talons, made the innocent query: "Do you suppose the bird swooped the mouse off the ground?"

Many people have come great distances to see the hawk migrations but, lacking time, or striking poor weather, they have departed in disappointment. I don't think I ever felt quite so much sympathy for anyone as I did for the Pathé News cameraman who descended upon the Sanctuary in the late fall of 1936, determined to make a sound film of the migrating hawks. I told the men that the only "sound" they might get would be that of the wind brushing through the hemlocks. The flight conditions happened to be at their worst, and I tried to prevail on the men to give up and to return another time. But they were sent out here from Manhattan by some hard-bitten executive, and pictures they must get. So with courage born of stubbornness, they unloaded their truck to tote all their heavy, back-breaking equipment to the crest of the mountain. Twice they did this, only to brave raw easterly winds and chilling mists; and they saw not a single hawk! Later I learned that the men, and their boss, had had the impression that swarms of hawks turned up daily about four o'clock to be fed. Fed what? Why, bread crumbs and possibly other table scraps!

The "hollyhock man" hailed from Allentown. He was a machinist, past middle age, with an uncontrollable desire to talk. With superb candor, he likened himself to a phonograph—one that could not run down. How did he happen into our wilderness? Well, like Johnny Appleseed, the "hollyhock man" had a mission: to beautify the country roads with garden flowers. He took a fancy to our mountain, and especially to our narrow, picturesque road. Would we like hollyhocks to plant, at the house and along the road? He said he could get *thousands* of the plants, enough to keep me busy turning turf and wielding a mattock for weeks on end. He visualized hollyhocks nodding and blinking all over the Sanctuary. So our friend turned up one day, his car loaded with great clumps of hollyhocks. It was useless to tell the fellow that he was wasting his time—and mine. I transplanted a few clumps, and invited him to dig in all that he could, which he started to do with vigor and spirit. Our rocky terrain finally exhausted his enthusiasm. He has not been back since the fall of 1946. Only four clumps of hollyhocks, which I planted myself, have survived to remind us of the "hollyhock man."

Several romances have also featured in the category of our adventures at Hawk Mountain. The one I like best also followed one of those knocks on Schaumboch's door. On a day in early spring a sweet and attractive Girl Scout executive came searching for a summertime camp site for her charges. In the course of several more visits, the young lady fell in love with the mountain, and in due time she attained her objective. But her sights were set much higher. . . .

About the same time a fine young bachelor of our acquaintance, disdaining the company of city girls whose lives revolved around hairdressers, movies and bridge, asked Irma whether we knew any girl who, like himself, enjoyed hiking, camping and other phases of outdoor life. "Why, certainly, we know just the girl for you, Bob," spoke up my wife with enormous assurance. For three months we tried in vain to synchronize the visits of this pair. Finally, on a Saturday evening in the hawking season, the twain did meet, in a group of some ten house guests. We staged an impromptu mock wedding in the kitchen, which was attended with uproarious hilarity on the part of our guests. The fun over,

Irma and I wondered whether we hadn't carried the joke too far. Bob and Ann were so embarrassed we scarcely heard a word from them the rest of the week end. But the stage was set, apparently. Love flourished as the weeks rolled by, during which they frequently enjoyed each other's company. Then, after another three months, we heard of the engagement. Ann was altogether smitten with her Lochinvar. We received a very tender message from them both, saying they were deeply in love; and they congratulated us on our signal success with our "lonely hearts club."

In the summer of 1947 we hillbillies took off for a change of scenery: a fortnight along the Virginia coast. A young couple from Long Island came to occupy Schaumboch's during our absence. It was an altogether happy arrangement, for this couple delighted in roaming the mountain and they enjoyed the novelty of staying in the ancient house. Mrs. D. later wrote to us that the house, the locale, our goats, and the general atmosphere reminded her of her childhood days in Switzerland. As a token of their appreciation of a pleasant holiday on Hawk Mountain, they sent Mrs. Edge a substantial check for the Sanctuary.

The next summer my wife and I made a trip to Maine, and we let another young couple from New York City have free use of the house for two weeks. But this couple were made of different stuff; a vacation at Atlantic City would have been just the thing for them, not the simplicities of our rugged mountain. In this case the young woman was most unhappy, just why we never did learn, but after a week of fretting and weeping her husband took her back to the city. We never received so much as a "thank-you" note from this pair.

Among the many notable personalities whom we have entertained at Schaumboch's, one stands out for his peculiar genius. We do not refer to Charles Schweinfurth's amazing ability to provide the botanical name for every plant of the fields and woods, nor do we refer to his knowledge of orchids, which probably exceeds that of any other man alive. The thing that makes Charlie so distinctive is his ability to recognize a twenty-minute boiled egg. The first morning that he and Henry Dunbar stayed with us, Charlie asked for a couple of twenty-minute boiled eggs for his breakfast. My wife and I thought this an extremely odd and amusing request. We both decided, however, that ten minutes would hard-boil any egg. At breakfast Charlie ate his eggs without a murmur.

The next morning Charlie called down from his room, "If it isn't too much trouble, will you *please* cook the eggs twenty minutes; they weren't done quite long enough yesterday." Charlie got his twenty-minute eggs, and I received a sober lesson in scientific exactitude. When our friends had departed, we found this clever limerick in our guest book, the work of Henry Dunbar:

> *"When asked how he wanted his egg,*
> *Charles replied: 'Twenty minutes, I beg;*
> *It's very delicious, and far more nutritious*
> *Though it burns up your gas by the keg.'"*

It is only natural that most of our visitors are on the receiving end of our contacts with them and the things they receive are usually much information, or very valuable time. (A naturalist is supposed to have no responsibilities and all the time in the world.) So it was a delightful surprise when a certain couple appeared at the Sanctuary one gloomy morning in November, 1947, not to receive, but to *give*. This couple had come eighty-five miles from Wilmington to see birds, but it began to rain, so they drove up to Schaumboch's, and there followed the inevitable knock on the door. In the course of a very pleasant and spirited conversation, we learned that it was the couple's wedding anniversary. Suddenly the young woman said to her husband: "Instead of the jewelry and trinkets you were going to give me, I'd rather that you give the equivalent in money to the Sanctuary." This was something new and different in the manner of social intercourse at Schaumboch's. Without batting an eyelash, the gentleman pulled a crisp fifty-dollar note from his billfold and presented it to us for the Sanctuary. It was all so spontaneous, so gracious, and so very generous that my wife and I were quite overwhelmed. Just before that the man had come in with an armful of beautiful yellow chrysanthemums, and these he heaped into my wife's arms. But the kind lady received a beautiful anniversary present anyway, for we took the couple to see Conrad Roland, the artist, who lives at the foot of the mountain, a few miles from the Sanctuary. There the generous husband purchased a beautiful portrait of waxwings for his charming wife. It rained happiness for everybody that day.

Death, too, has stalked across the scenes of recent Hawk Mountain history. I remember the party of deer-hunters that was poaching along the south bounds of the Sanctuary a number of years ago. One of the men tripped on a root, his gun went off, instantly killing the nearest person, a boy of fourteen years. The deer-hunting party turned into a funeral procession, moving hopelessly down the road.

Just before the war, a young insurance salesman, tiring of the ceaseless struggle and burdened with debt, took the easiest way out. He must have been dead two days when we discovered him, on the west end of the Sanctuary road, slumped over his wheel with a bullet in his head. Hundreds of people had been coming up the mountain to seek pleasure and inspiration; this unfortunate chap came to end it all. His body was reported to the police by Mrs. Richard C. Doty, of Reading, one of our members, who forthwith was taken into custody and held for hours as a material witness!

In the late fall of 1945 a Navy fighter plane crashed into our mountain in heavy weather. The pilot was killed, the co-pilot escaped miraculously, but with severe wounds. Schaumboch's became headquarters for the State Police and other officials while rescue work proceeded, and an inch of mud accumulated on the newly laid floors. I was overseas at the time. Professor Trembley, then in charge of the Sanctuary, had to cope with the mobs of the morbidly curious who were attracted instantly like ants to a disturbed ant-hill. Since then every schoolboy within ten miles has sought out the wrecked plane for souvenirs.

We have many campers in our midst during the summer and fall; they are a harmless lot generally, and give us little cause for concern. The inevitable exception appeared in the form of a tall, nervous youth from a nearby city, who came to camp for a few days, and to scare the daylights out of my wife. It happened during a quiet mid-week in June, while I was away in the Poconos, and the teen-age camper and Irma were the only people on the mountain. Irma, ever hospitable, and particularly so where young people are concerned, invited the lad in to have luncheon with her. During the course of the meal the boy told my wife in glowing detail how he was taught by his father to kill woodchucks by waiting for the creatures as they emerged from their dens, then grabbing and strangulating the poor animals. From there on he monopolized the conversation, skipping from one gory act to another.

The boy's obsession with killing fanned the instinct of fear in my wife, and for the first time in all our years on Hawk Mountain she felt chills run down her spine. There was something about this strange boy and his obvious relish at the recital of brutal deeds to animals, that finally unnerved Irma.

My wife and I had been in the habit of sleeping in one of the shelters, the one which was temporarily used by our sanguinary visitor, who fully expected Irma to turn in, in due time, on her side of the shelter, where our bedding was laid out. The lad retired much earlier than did my wife. But Irma had decided that she'd sleep a lot better right in the house, with all the doors locked. At ten minutes to two she awoke from an uneasy slumber, with forebodings. At exactly two o'clock the stillness of the night was shattered by a terrific pounding and beating as of a club against boards. As the noise continued Irma remembered that the cellar door might not be bolted, so she flew to the cellar and breathlessly took care of that situation. Then she returned to the attic-bedroom and waited fearfully, with the kerosene light turned low, for whatever might happen. But quietness returned to the lonely mountain-top. In the morning, having lost her fear, she asked the boy how he slept. "Didn't hear a thing," said he. When she mentioned the frightful pounding from the shelter at the unearthly hour of two o'clock, the boy exclaimed with a look of great surprise: "Oh, could you hear that!"

Later on, after some prodding, the boy sheepishly confessed to Irma that a wood rat, or some other small trespasser, had tangled with his bedding, rousing him from sleep. Panicky, he seized a handy piece of firewood and pounded everything within reach. The four-footed intruder scampered to safety; the boy calmly went back to sleep; but Irma, trembling in her room, thought that her life had hung by a thread!

There have been ever so many young men—it is not easy to recall them all—to whom Hawk Mountain has meant much in terms of bird-watching, peace, beauty and good fellowship.

Among the earliest of our young visitors was sixteen-year-old Sam Guss. He used to hitch-hike from his home in Reading. He planted small patches of buckwheat and millet for the birds, and he also made nest boxes and erected them near Schaumboch's. Sam is now a highly successful veterinarian.

Albert Conway was another high school lad who found his way to the Sanctuary. He was largely responsible for the creation, in 1940, of the Isaac Robert's Memorial Shelter (donated by the West Chester Bird Club). Albert, a first-rate ornithologist, is professionally a psychologist, teaching at a near-by university. Scott Dearolf, always spirited and as keen as a falcon, turns up regularly to perform all manner of good deeds for us. Nor can we praise too highly James Deetz and Walton Robey, who traveled by bus and shanks' mare an entire night from Cumberland, Maryland (270 miles), to see a hawk flight. Their interest in the Sanctuary became so great that they craved to spend a summer with us. They put in eight weeks of hard work with me, performing man-sized tasks which might have discouraged less valiant spirits.

Long before the war, Ben Goodwin and Bill Fricke used to come to the Sanctuary from their homes near Philadelphia. Thanks to Ben's ingenuity and to the prodigious efforts of both boys, a telephone was rigged up atop the ridge (two-thirds of a mile), which enabled us, in the fall of 1942, to conduct original speed-of-flight experiments with the migrating hawks. Our results were subsequently published in *The Auk*. Ben and Bill, Bob Geigler and Dave Fitts, all of them youths of unusual promise and tremendously devoted to the Sanctuary, lost their lives in the war. Two of our shelters have been dedicated to the memory of these boys.

Among the many young people who have come to us when we needed them were Elmer and Eileen Swartley of Kintnersville, Pennsylvania. They spent a delayed honeymoon camping on the mountain six weeks during one busy fall.

Without their help my wife and I would have been hopelessly plowed under with work. And Tommy Hanson, of Reading, a keen young ornithologist, has been carrying on where some of our older friends, now widely scattered, left off.

Bert Schaughency, his vivacious wife Millie, Bob Lorber, and Charlie Haynes, all of East Orange, have also been a great boon to us. Their special contribution to the Sanctuary was the acquisition and installation of a permanent telephone system connecting Schaumboch's with the entrance and the Lookout: a three-way hookup with two miles of field wire, which enables us to keep things nicely under control, including the hazard of fire.

These are but a few of the people whose lives have touched ours like spring sunshine—people with whom we have felt the "grasp of fellowship," which has been our deepest satisfaction, our greatest reward.

CHAPTER 11

WINTER
ISOLATION

Our nearest neighbor is two miles to the east, near the foot of the mountain, and an unbroken wilderness void of human beings extends four and a half miles south, to the nearest town, Hamburg. We have no telephone and no electricity. We have never felt it a hardship to be without these amenities to living. Despite our oil lamps, despite the washtub in which we bathed with hot water dipped from the tank on the kitchen stove, we have lived well.

Our detachment from the world in these times of endless turmoil and crises intrigues some of our friends; they envy our "splendid isolation." Of course we are not as remote as some might think, for people from all over the continent, and at least fifteen foreign countries, nosing their cars up our mountain road eight months of the year, have enriched our lives. Often we are asked: "Aren't you lonely up there?" We reply emphatically, "No! there's never a dull moment." Not even in the depth of winter, when deep snow closes the road and we seldom see visitors, have we ever felt the slightest touch of loneliness.

A young truck driver once delivered cement to us and thought it remarkable that anyone could live up here on the mountain. Then he saw one of our goats, and exclaimed: "At least, you got something human up here!"

I am a lucky fellow, for it would go hard with me if my wife demanded to be taken to night clubs, or to the movies, or to bridge parties, or if she dashed off at every trumpet call of the Womens' Political League. We are very simple people, with simple habits, free from the distractions which most people crave—or endure.

We enjoy people, but we also enjoy solitude—especially the solitude of the mountains in winter. This would be an unthinkable existence to the mass of people. I remember the woman who came to get her young son who had been staying with us. She could not get off the mountain quickly enough. "You can have it," she said tartly, "I'll take Atlantic City."

It is one of the tragedies of modern civilization, I think, that most people are unable to enjoy solitude. When I was in the Service I observed that almost all the stalwart young heroes whom I encountered were quite unable to endure solitude; indeed, they seemed to be afraid to be alone with their thoughts. Because I enjoyed solitary excursions into the jungles of the South Pacific islands I was considered eccentric. For perhaps a million years man must have been forced into solitude from time to time; his nervous system became attuned to the stimuli of nature: the sound of the wind, the lapping of waters, the green of plant life. Such things soothe the nervous system, allowing imagination and constructive thoughts to ripen in the individual. Christ, and all the truly great figures of history, recognized the value of solitude; they were able to pull themselves onto the right spiritual track by frequent contact with nature. So it is that because modern man has, for the most part, lost the ability to use solitude, he is quite unaware of the things he suffers. Perhaps a Sanctuary like ours has an additional function: to provide solitude and re-creation for the human soul.

As a youngster, city-bred, I yearned for the simplicities of country life; not merely rural living, but far-off wilderness living. I wanted to escape from the grating noises, the confusion, the artificialities of the city; I wanted to get as far as possible from the slavery of our machine civilization. I was inspired by Thoreau, who wrote: ". . . if one advances confidently in the direction of his dreams, and endeavors to live the life which he has imagined, he will meet with a success unexpected in common hours." I enjoyed my first taste of solitude during three years passed in the pioneer development of the Pleasant Valley Bird Sanctuary in the heart of the Berkshires. It was a salutary experience for me, in which I quickly learned the full meaning of self-reliance. For to breast the sudden transition from city living to life in the woods meant learning how to use my hands and tools. I then in part had achieved my dreams but, unlike Thoreau, I was a sorry bachelor. Three winters of complete aloneness could not entirely fulfill the "direction of my dreams." I wanted a marriage partner, but I despaired of ever finding one who would put up with me. But as all things supposedly come to him who waits, in due time I found my wife during another three years of comparative solitude on Cape Cod.

We have spent five winters on Hawk Mountain (two of them before the war), without ever once feeling any trace of "cabin fever." To both of us, winter is a season of deep contentment. And nearly complete isolation. We have been snowed in as much as seven weeks at a time. Once only have we seen a snowplow on our usually forgotten road. That was after a severe storm in late January, 1948—the winter which, according to the oldest inhabitants of the valley, was the worst and hardest in their memory. Except for the little runways of our dogs and our own imprints around the house, the snow lay deep and trackless. And then, wonder of wonders, the snowplow churned up the road. We could hardly believe our eyes. For a brief hour or so, we were excited and delighted with this consideration never shown to us before.

But presently we reconsidered. We resented this intrusion! We were blissfully secure in our isolation. The unbroken road was beautiful. Who cared for a life-line to civilization!

Our winter preparations begin in late May, when the tender shoots of pokeweed, or pigeon-berry, appear along the roadside. The pokeweed shoots are delicious; like asparagus, but better, in my opinion. Pokeweed grows so abundantly near Schaumboch's that my wife cans quarts of it. She has also canned dandelion greens. It is a thrilling thing, in the dead of winter, to bring up from the cellar these tasty, nourishing Maytime products. Then, in June and July, she busily gathers and preserves the wild strawberries and blackberries (from the valley pastures), and the vegetables from our gardens. Later she makes the most savory jellies from the wild grapes which grow in dense tangles all about the edges of our little apple orchard.

By early September the cellar food shelves neatly display many jars of garden products. The coalbin is full, and wood is stacked high. But we are far from self-sufficient, since we have very little arable land and a minimum of livestock. Our livestock consist of a pair of Saanen goats, which provide us with all the milk we need throughout the year, and some Rhode Island roosters. Our small patch of open land provides ample pasturage for the goats. We have been able to cut enough hay from this land to carry the goats through a part of the winter, but the hay must be supplemented with much alfalfa, which we buy from our farmer friends in the valley. The roosters often trouble our slumbers, for they crow lustily throughout the night as well as all day. They are such gorgeously colored, spirited creatures, lording it over our dogs, that it requires great resolution to translate them into steaming, succulent Sunday dinners. Incidentally, the roosters have complete freedom throughout the summer and fall, yet we have not lost a single one to predatory birds and animals.

Sub-zero temperatures seldom strike the mountain. The house, situated in a dimple of the mountain, at 1100 feet, is exposed to the easterly gales, but it is reasonably well protected from the north and west. On only three occasions during the bitter winter of 1948 did the mercury at the house dip to just below zero. But in the Great Valley, where the cold air settles like a heavy blanket, the temperatures often sagged to as much as 18° or 20° below zero. On the other hand, the snow is usually gone from the valley floor, which is about 500 feet above sea level, by mid-March; and on the mountain it lingers into April.

Ice storms visit us three or four times each winter. Though they may spread across the mountain a sparkling, crystal mantle whose beauty beggars description, they are nevertheless the only dreaded features of our winter; they invariably spell real *ice-olation,* and sometimes wreak havoc to the forest. During the winter of 1947 there was a three-weeks' period when we could hardly move from the house, for to venture out on the glassy road or into the woods was an invitation to a broken neck. Yet 300 yards down the road, at an elevation of about 750 feet, there is a sharp line of demarcation, below which there is seldom any ice.

One Christmas Eve a furious ice storm struck. Sleet and snow piled up rapidly and a stinging east wind crackled the ice-burdened birches by the house. We were snug by the little wood stove in our living room. There was an odd scratching at the window. "Sleet," I remarked to my wife. The scratching persisted. Upon investigation we saw a small bird struggling against the windowpane. I went out and gently picked up a goldfinch. It might have perished within an hour, on the deep snow of the window sill. The goldfinch had room and board for the night, in a small wire cage which

I placed in the cool, dark attic. Next morning we looked out on a glittering, fairyland world in which we were trapped securely. But not our goldfinch. It took off with a joyous song. Nothing could have given us deeper pleasure on that Christmas Day than the rescue of that terror-stricken little bird, lost in the night.

The ice storm of New Year's Day, 1948, will long be remembered. The devastation to trees, to telephone and electric installations throughout the Northeast was terrific, and brought with it real hardship to thousands of families. Though we were locked in as though in the heart of a glacier, we were not inconvenienced. Our friends in the valley, long accustomed to electrical conveniences, dug out their old oil lamps, put aside their radios, and for a month or more reverted to the simple ways of fifty years ago. At Schaumboch's, our oil lamps and coal and wood stoves glowed cheerfully, and our battery-set radio kept us up to the minute on all the crucial happenings between man and weather. But the inch-and-a-half wall of ice that formed on our mountain literally crushed the forest, destroying or damaging most of the first-rate hardwood trees. It was ghastly. The rattling of the ice-sheathed branches sounded like the clashing of steel sabres.

Throughout that night we were awakened by the sharp, pistol-like sounds of branches and trees snapping under their burdens of accumulated ice. The next morning we could hardly believe our eyes. We looked out through ice-draped windows on an incredible world of ice and splintery trees bowed to the ground, of small trees flattened, of mangled trees everywhere—a frozen chaos! All day the impenetrable woods resounded with the cracking and snapping of oaks and poplars. I was awed to see a big poplar, and a fifty-foot oak, each snap into splinters, like matchsticks. The top of our big persimmon tree went and the tree looked as though it had been pruned by a maniac. Nearly every large tree about the house sustained ugly, irremediable damage. Interlacing branches and tops of trees folded over and settled athwart the road, making it impassable.

Snow, and chickadees all that day! The chickadees, bless their sturdy little souls, slid from icicle to icicle to reach the feeding stations which were well stocked with everything a chickadee loves. I heard a pileated woodpecker hammering (or chopping ice!) south of the house.

The radio was full of talk of the storm's havoc—"the worst storm of the century," with power lines down, trees littering all highways, motor traffic almost nil, and rampant devastation from Maine to Missouri. The ice of this one storm clung to the east side of Schaumboch's for six weeks.

A week later a gang of roadmen cleared our road of the storm-slashed trees. It required three days for twelve men to remove the debris from a three-mile stretch of the road. And as late as January 9th we heard the snapping and the crashing of trees. For days the sun was in hiding. We would look out the window and wince with pain: gray, icy fog hanging like doom over a forest that looked as though it had been ravaged by war; chilling, clinging fog, producing a lost-world effect. Then, at last, eight days after the storm, the sun came out, coyly, tentatively, exposing diamond-studded horizons. The ice-armored trees took on sparkling life and lustre; a dead, gray world was transformed into matchless brilliance and beauty—but a beauty cruel and pain-inspired.

Bird life on our mountain, so excitingly abundant in the periods of migration, drops to its nadir during the winter months. Then far more birds may be found on the farmlands along the foot of the mountain, where there is a greater variety of natural foods, including weed-seeds. But our two pairs of "log-cocks" (pileated woodpeckers) are worth two hundred common birds. For three consecutive winters one pair has been wedded to the vicinity of Schaumboch's. Several times a week we are thrilled to hear the wild cry of one or the other of these big woodpeckers, and sometimes we see them in flight over the orchard.

Our experiences with ruffed grouse would be hard to duplicate elsewhere. In the winter the grouse come to feast on the buds of the poplar trees or on the sumac, visible from our kitchen windows. We have watched as many as four grouse in one tree, feasting with patrician decorum. Grouse have been abundant on our mountain, but the deadly ice storms of the winter of 1948 depleted their numbers as effectively as though the birds had been caught in the grip of an epidemic plague.

Once we could write, as did Thomas Morton in Massachusetts, in 1632, "turkies . . . at divers times have sallied by our doores." Before the war it was not unusual for us to see three or four wild turkeys fairly near the house, sometimes strolling in the road. Many a winter's morning we found their tracks in the snow. But alas! we no longer have wild turkeys. I am afraid they were killed off during the war years when we were away and the Sanctuary was inadequately protected.

Chickadees help to make our winters at Hawk Mountain exciting. "A single chickadee will draw the sting from any winter morning," wrote Charles C. Abbott. I have studied birds from Maine to Mexico, and when I served with the Navy in the Pacific Islands, I made the acquaintance of many brilliantly-plumaged, exotic birds of the jungle; but none have ever given me more delight that the chickadee, that little "scrap of valor." In fair weather and foul, you will find chickadees bobbing about cheerfully, confidently and sociably with their fellows. The chickadee has always been my favorite bird. One winter a number of years ago two chickadees flew down to a chunk of suet I held between my teeth. The fearless little birds clamped their feet on my lips and pecked vigorously at the food, while I stood motion-less yet so excited I was ready to burst. On other occasions I have had chickadees light on my hat and also on my out-stretched hand, which contained sunflower seeds or suet. When I worked for Edward Howe Forbush he generously allowed me to write the biography of the chickadee for his great work on birds. It was one of the greatest honors I have known.

Ten chickadees bounced among our food trays every morn-ing during the winter of 1947; they liked our bounty so much that seven of them were back the next winter, joined by four newcomers. Most of these returned the winter of 1949, bring-ing their kith and kin, which numbered fifteen new birds. The latter are readily discerned, trapped, and given tiny alu-minum bands furnished by the Fish and Wildlife Service. Our chickadees deserve nothing but the best. In return for their friendly ways and the pleasure they bring us daily, we pro-vide suet, sunflower seeds, doughnuts and peanut butter—great gobs of it on whole wheat bread. Some of our chicka-dees have year-round lodgings in the nesting boxes in the orchard. There are many chickadees scattered over the mountain, but the lucky birds at the house surely live the life of Riley.

Redpolls—very rare in our region—spent the winter of 1947 with us. I first saw the dainty little finches at the Look-out on a brilliant day in early January. A major event, and a very exciting one! It had been ten years since I had seen any of these gregarious wanderers from the Far North. Some 300 redpolls were swarming among the birches, feeding on the catkins, and with them were a score of siskins and a few goldfinches. The next day, and almost every morning there-after, until March 9th, they flocked about the house, usually late in the forenoon. Each morning's visit brought fresh excitement. On a Sunday morning in late January, I tramped through our woods, avoiding the glare-ice road, to enjoy a ten-mile hike in the valley, hoping to see large numbers of birds. Imagine my delight upon returning to the house at noon to find far more birds than I had seen on my long walk. Redpolls covered two apple trees; they swarmed in the road, gleaning grit from the coal-ashes; they fluttered on the ice-encrusted snow picking up the seeds of the birches; and, most surprising, at least fifty of the hardy little birds were bathing and wading in the icy water of the tiny brook by the house. The temperature was 38°. The bathers then flew up to the apple trees and shook and flashed their feathers, chattering contentedly in low tones. There was so much natural food for them, and their companions the siskins, that they ignored our well-stocked food trays.

Juncos and tree sparrows, birds of the weedy fields and town-borders during the winter months, were our guests in the winter of 1948. They promptly took over the lunch counters and enjoyed our largesse so much that they lingered long after their valley brethren had departed for the north. A lone junco, the first to discover our aerie, must have been famished. A doughnut was its lifesaver! The bird chiseled away at the doughnut for fifteen minutes uninterruptedly, ignoring the protestations of the chickadees, who considered the doughnut their own property. Three days later a second junco turned up—our first winter juncos on Hawk Mountain. At the same time, a sextette of tree sparrows arrived, all ravenous and all dominating the food trays the first afternoon. One bird lingered until darkness, gorging on millet seed. Thereafter it was nip and tuck at the trays between chickadees and tree sparrows. Only our downy woodpeckers fed in peace.

One January a saw-whet owl, another rare visitor to our region, spent at least a week with us, though we did not see it. Just before dusk it would call *whurdle, whurdle, whurdle* in softly modulated tones. This voice in the wilderness would have haunted and mystified us had I not become well acquainted, years ago in New England, with this delightful pigmy among owls.

A pair of great horned owls serenade us with their resonant hooting on many late afternoons throughout the fall and winter. They are responsive birds and usually answer readily when I call to them, using my cupped hands through which I blow. I would not think of having my supper without first communing with the owls, who sound off from the vicinity of the Lookout. I feel a special bond of sympathy and affection for our resident "hoot owls," on which the State has ignominiously set a bounty of five dollars per head, a sordid bargain for the irreplaceable symbol of the pervading wilderness spirit.

I can claim with the Psalmist that "I know all the fowls of the mountains; and the wild beasts of the field are mine." Our animal life during the winter months is far more varied and numerous than the bird life, but it is less obvious and must often be read and interpreted in the record of the snow. The winter begins with a large number of deer frequenting the Sanctuary. They come to us in early December, in the course of the detested deer-hunting season. I have often seen deer leaping over our boundary wire and into the Sanctuary when the surrounding forest was creeping with deer-hunters. By midwinter most of the deer have taken off for the sheltered ravines and rhododendron tangles of the lower flanks of the ridge, or to the proximity of the open fields. At least a score are residents, however. We have seen the deer stalk out of the woods in the gathering twilight and come to feast at our persimmon tree, pawing and shaking the lower branches to get at the fruit.

Gray squirrels and opossums also come to enjoy their share of the persimmons. The squirrels fearlessly spend long hours in the topmost part of the tree, where the fruit is abundant. The raccoons that help the robins to strip the big cherry tree in back of the house during June remind us of their neighborliness during the inclement season when, on mild days, we find their tracks quite close to the house. The timorous cottontail rabbit is everywhere, often in the most surprising places in the woods; but they also build their nests in the orchard and raise their young in spite of the daily trespass of our dogs. I suspect the perennial presence of our owls is possible only because of the ubiquitous cottontails and wood rats. A tramp through the woods nearly always reveals the presence of foxes, both the red and the gray. I have often in winter examined the faeces of the red fox, and invariably they have contained the remains of mice. Neither species is numerous, for in all the surrounding country the unfortunate creatures are harried and trapped relentlessly.

Red-backed mice and short-tailed shrews occasionally seek food right at our kitchen door. Marvelously alert little beasts, they can disappear into their snow-tunnels as fast as you can flick an eyelid. Some of the smaller furry creatures of the woods invade Schaumboch's regularly. White-footed mice are among the most winsome and attractive and courageous little animals that I know, but I prefer them in their own world, rather than when they intrude into ours. When they invade the house I set traps reluctantly. I have endeavored vainly to make the cellar walls mouse-proof. But the mice come, and we must keep controlling them everlastingly, or else suffer an endless repertoire of mouse-noises within our thick stone walls. A weasel took over the job of control for us in the late fall of 1947, for which I was grateful. It lived in a stone wall by our garden. His mousing activities were so wonderfully effective that we were practically free of mice all that winter. The weasel's work was further abetted, I am sure, by both short-tailed shrews and the tiny smoky shrews which also take up residence in our cellar.

Alleghany wood rats and occasionally bats were former inhabitants of Schaumboch's, which we once tolerated, for they did help to enliven two of our earlier winters at the Sanctuary. When we renovated the old house and improved the cellar with a concrete floor, in the spring of 1946, all our relations with the rats ceased, for no self-respecting wood rat would deign to dwell with us. We have no regrets!

Our daily contact with the birds and animals leading their untrammeled lives has brightened our own lives immeasurably. There are men who earn their sustenance as "game protectors." But they must not be confused with animal lovers. The game protector is a breed I know well. Rarely does he have humility and love in his heart for the creatures of the wild. He slays the fox to save the rabbit; he kills the owl hoping to fill the hunter's bag with more partridges; and he resists and stamps out anything that might compete with the pleasures of the hunter. And rarely does he understand, or even care to understand, the delicate, complex inter-relationships of all wild things. The game protector is the minion of the hunter. And as Samuel Johnson has observed, "It is very strange and melancholy that the paucity of human pleasures should persuade us ever to call hunting one of them."

A typical winter's day at Schaumboch's begins shortly after daybreak. I skip down to the kitchen, perk up the coal range, start a wood fire in the living-room stove. Then I get breakfast—my special province—while Irma goes out to milk and tend the goats and feed the chickens. Upon her return with the rich, creamy milk of which she is always proud, breakfast is ready and leisurely consumed, while we may listen to John

Gambling's "Sense, news, music and nonsense" over the radio.

Though we may be detached from the world, the current of our lives moves quickly; we are sufficient unto ourselves, no two days are alike, and each passing day brings its own flavor and satisfactions.

After breakfast there are always household chores to be done and a half hour stint with the cross-cut saw. Regardless of the weather, I spend at least a half hour each day with axe and saw; keeping muscularly toned and in trim is as important to me as getting the firewood; one act complements the other. Irma used to saw wood with me until one day she quit, with the explanation, "I don't want to be a boy any more!" And since then she has devoted her spare time to more creative work, such as rug-making. She is extremely versatile. She does all the interior house painting and wall papering, with professional results. If the weather is pleasant, I may check on our bounds or take a long tramp through the woods with the dogs; Irma sometimes accompanies me. Or I may prune the orchard trees.

If the snow is not too deep, I enjoy hard physical work outdoors. During the winter of 1947, without any help I logged from our own woods some eighty stout chestnut poles with which to make a three-rail rustic fence. That same winter, with the help of Jake Kunkel, a local carpenter, I built a badly-needed back porch to Schaumboch's, and an Adirondack shelter for the use of the campers who throng to the Sanctuary in the summer and fall. Our friend Jake, a small but extremely solid man of roughhewn features, is a rare personality. His workmanship is of the highest calibre, with never any lost motion. He asks only ninety cents an hour, an amazingly low wage in these times for a skilled carpenter. And Jake must "make a showing" for each day's work, else he is unhappy.

Correspondence and writing consume much of my time. My weekly (sometimes semi-weekly) walks to the mailbox at the end of the rural route in Eckville net me forty to fifty letters, each of which I try to answer before the next trip. To save time, I have learned to acknowledge as many letters as possible on a postal card. My correspondents sometimes overestimate my abilities. A woman sent me an S. O. S. in midwinter for "some worms or some kind of food" to keep alive a "baby bird" she had rescued. A gentleman from Toronto wrote, requesting me to find and reserve a cottage for him and his family in anticipation of a visit to the Sanctuary in the fall. And I have received requests for literature or information from points as widely separated as Alaska and England. All in all, my correspondence is a stimulating adventure in itself.

During the late winter of 1948, my visits to the mailbox were made by sled, an ordinary child's sled. Once, I negotiated the two and a half miles from the house to the mailbox in six minutes—like the speed of a comet, with only my tail visible as I ended up in a snow bank, with head and shoulders completely buried. My wife and I have as much fun as any ten-year-olds, coasting on the turns and steep grades near the house. A sled, we have found, is an indispensable adjunct to fun on the mountain.

In the late afternoon of a sunshiny day, it is pleasant to look out of our east windows, at the chickadees getting their supper at the feeding trays; and, beyond, at the long view down the valley. This, to use John Burroughs' phrase, is the "ripest hour of the day." The sun disappears early over the white crest of the mountain, pulling a long shadow across the Sanctuary, but we see the flush of sunset an hour later, reflected glowingly from the windows of the farmhouses. It is a mellow moment, made for meditation; it is the time to count our blessings and give thanks for the peace and simplicities that are our daily enjoyment.

In the evening, if we should feel the need of a change of scenery or of atmosphere, we "dine out." Our procedure is simple and effective. We arrange a table in the living room, provoke the wood fire to a ruddy glow, light a candle, and don our "city clothes." Irma brings in the food. And then we enjoy our make-believe, imagining people at tables all about us. Irma makes wisecracks about the ladies' hats and shoes, recalling some of the odd combinations she sees at the gate during the fall; I nod and make agreeable conversation, and put on my best manners; and we continue our whimsey, with huge enjoyment, until it is time to listen to Lowell Thomas. Then we are pulled back to reality by the generally grim recital of the news of the world.

We can dispense with most of the gadgets and the material things with which many people burden their lives, but I do not think we would willingly be without our radio. For much as we rejoice in our winter sequestration, we yet like to open a window, as it were, and look out upon the world. The radio enables us to do just that. I think that the miracle of the radio is taken too much for granted by most people. We are inclined to accept its highest good, as well as its perversions, as a matter of course. No matter how much trash and tinsel the "window" may look out upon, there are vistas, none the less, that are varied and sweet, and often inspiring. The long winter evenings are enriched by the mere turning of a dial. We may attend the provocative discussions of the Town Meeting of the Air; or we may listen ecstatically to the Boston Symphony Orchestra; or we may tune in on a juicy, spine-prickling murder mystery, the compliments of the Inner Sanctum. On a Saturday afternoon, we attend the Metropolitan Opera; I anticipate this eagerly from week to week, but not so my wife, who was ready to commit mayhem on me after I had subjected her to the "screams" of *Madame Butterfly* for an entire afternoon. We also delight in the dramatic performances of the Theatre Guild of the Air. And on late Monday evenings there is "My Friend Irma"—a half hour of hilarious, wholesome nonsense. The radio program that gives us the greatest pleasure, I think, for its whole-heartedness and skillful handling of all kinds of personalities, is *Welcome Travelers,* featured from Chicago with the inimitable Tommy Bartlett.

Our radio entertainment seldom exceeds fifteen hours each week, and claims but a small part of our evenings, which are more likely to be spent absorbed in books or magazines, or writing letters to friends. We are omnivorous readers, and reading, sometimes to each other, is one of our greatest pleasures. Years ago I used to read an average of two books a week, but a busy life long since upset that schedule. Now I am lucky if I can find time to read two books a month.

When the evening is nearly spent, and before we bank the fire in the kitchen stove, we may go out into the frosty night. We pick our way silently up the snow-hushed road to the crest of the mountain. In the distant valleys glow the friendly town lights; above gleam the austere, celestial lights. Darkness and light reign alike, in profound peace. On a moonlit night the glittering snow is etched with lacy shadow-patterns from the leafless trees. We may not say a word until we are near the house, for to return is like leaving a cathedral in which a loud word is a profanation, or an irrelevant thought a sacrilege. Living close to nature, participating in her mysteries, we are aware of God on every hand-embodied in the landscape and identified in the animals and birds, the trees and rocks, in clouds and sunshine, with all of which we identify ourselves humbly, but with deep contentment and peace. This, I think, is the essence of religion. And it is our life in winter on Hawk Mountain.

PART THREE

"Doth the hawk fly by thy wisdom, and stretch her wings toward the south?"—Job 39:26

HAWKS ALOFT: THE FACTS AND FIGURES OF OUR FLYWAY

CHAPTER 12

The obstacles and trials we faced almost daily that first season of 1934, when the curtain was raised on the drama of Hawk Mountain, were offset by the novelty of the hawk migrations. Never before had I seen more than forty or fifty hawks in an entire year of active birding. Now it was almost commonplace to see that many hawks—with a few eagles for good measure—in a matter of minutes; and it was not unusual to see a few hundred hawks of eight or ten species in one day. Exciting? Thrilling? Why, that would be putting it mildly. The spectacular migrations of the "aristocrats of the air" got into my blood, like a virus. The first two seasons I would often reach the Lookout shortly after daybreak. I was slow in learning to curb my enthusiasm, to conserve my energy. Even when the flight conditions were excellent, the show seldom began before eight o'clock, I discovered eventually. Anyway, I couldn't bear the thought of missing a single bird. I just had to see the whole show! Looking back on those early days, I marvel that my wife was so tolerant of her zany husband.

It was no wonder that, having been smitten so badly with the hawking virus, I literally ate, drank and dreamed the fascinating facts of our hawk flyway—little hawks, big hawks, medium-sized hawks, all kinds of hawks curving down the

143

wall of the knife-edged ridge—a glorious procession of free-dom-possessed travelers.

I have perched on the Lookout rocks for more than 7,200 hours, in all kinds of weather, when the sun of early September sent the mercury soaring to 115°, and well into December, even as the clean, sharp blasts of Old Boreas drove all but a few hardy crows from the skies. Much of the time the birding, or the lack of birding, has been shared with countless visitors. However, I have spent many an exhilarating hour with the mountain, the clouds, the rocks and the birds all to myself. But let's talk about the weather . . . .

In the fall of the year at Hawk Mountain one may see hawks in every conceivable kind of weather short of rain. But I can assure you that the hawking can be terrifically exciting, or it can be terribly dull, depending on one little item in the weather—and that is WIND. The wind may come from any quarter so long as there is wind, but it takes a good, spanking nor'wester to produce dependable flights. No wind, no hawks summarizes flight conditions along our flyway.

Yet, on our "magic mountain," exceptions to every rule are translated into wondrous happenings. Example: September 16, 1940 was a quiet, windless day; a light curtain of mist hung over the terrain. There was scarcely a movement of any kind of bird life, till nearly eleven o'clock, when 32 broad-wings appeared, very low, to break the monotony. In the next five minutes a compact, whirling mass of broad-wings loomed over the Lookout; they mounted up and up in a gyrating, globular mass till they gained elevation, when they strung out loosely, revealing 504 birds in the group. Then, within twenty-two minutes, three other groups did the same thing. I saw a total of 1,112 broad-wings. And nothing went by the rest of that day! My friend, Earnest C. Baker, of Reading, was on hand that morning, but he did not see a single hawk; he had departed from the Sanctuary only a few minutes before this spectacular performance.

The *least favorable* winds are those from easterly and southerly quarters. When the wind is from these directions, observers at the Lookout usually strain their vision to the utmost, for the air-borne travelers show a tendency to avoid Hawk Mountain. The hawks may leave the ridge to take a short-cut far out across the valley to a spur of the ridge known as "The Pinnacle," four miles distant; then they may continue their passage along the south side of the spur. If the birds take this short-cut too far out, and if the visibility is poor, they may escape observation altogether. On the other hand, easterly or southerly winds sometimes bring the birds directly over the Sanctuary, but well to the south of the Lookout. At such times we may enjoy good hawking along the Sanctuary road, at the entrance, and even at Schaumboch's, the Sanctuary headquarters. Thus, in pre-Sanctuary days, the shotgun squads occasionally enjoyed their "sport" along the road; hence the tremendous accumlations of empty cartridges that we found there upon our arrival in early September, 1934.

It may be interesting to recall two or three instances when the wind was, generally speaking, "wrong." During the morning of September 13, 1946, many hawks passed far out over the valley. We were fortunate to see 200 birds from the Lookout. Late that afternoon, however, more than 400 broad-wings and 2 bald eagles put on a show directly over the house before they passed toward the southwest. On September 23, 1947, a day of clear, calm skies, a party of twelve observers spent a dull hawking day at the Lookout, although all admitted that the wonderful variety of small birds made up for the lack of hawks. About four o'clock, with a score of only twenty hawks for the day, we decided to leave. And just then a fresh wind sprang up in the south. As some of us reached the road we looked up, and to our amazement there were broad-wings streaming over at every elevation, some just over the treetops. In less than five minutes we counted 343 birds! Fred and Ellen Luden, of Reading, came out of the woods in time to see another 300 birds in the next few minutes. It was exciting to stand there, at the entrance, watching this procession of hawks which we very nearly missed completely! The most extraordinary hawk flight in the history of the Sanctuary occurred on the *worst* wind (a raw easterly) on September 16, 1948. For once the sky was literally black with the passage of many thousands of hawks that could be seen anywhere along the Sanctuary road. But of this amazing flight, more anon, in the next chapter. Suffice it to say, even an ill wind can blow some good at Hawk Mountain.

To really appreciate what the *right* wind will produce, almost unfailingly, let us consider October, 1939. Northerly winds prevailed on 20 days, and we tallied 10,476 hawks for that period—an average of 523.8 per day! By contrast, the whole of October, 1947, with its phenomenally balmy windless weather, brought only 2,171 hawks—an average of 77.6 per day (for 28 days of observation). We had but 3 days of northerly winds all that month.

It is now perfectly well known to amateurs and experts alike that the hawks—nature's original master gliders—concentrate in migration along the windward side of places like our Kittatinny Ridge, to ride the air currents. Without the wind striking against the flanks of the ridge, there can be no powerful updrafts of air upon which the birds coast in their effortless fashion, as do motorless gliders. Indeed, glider planes on more than one occasion have followed the same course as the drifting hawk. In 1937, an expert soaring pilot, Lewin B. Barringer, guided his high-performance sailplane on the updrafts the length of the Kittatinny Ridge for 160 miles, from Ellenville, N. Y., to a point near Harrisburg.

The Eastern Canadian Provinces, New York and New England form the vast reservoir from which come the birds of prey that use our ridge—one of the main migration highways for these birds. Thus at the appointed season, the hosts of hawks, making use of the uplifting air currents (and also the thermal currents) make their way with a minimum of effort, as though on an invisible roller coaster, eventually riding into the southern Appalachian region and beyond. For the most part, our ridge is broad, like the shoulders of a giant, so that the hawk flights are difficult to follow; but at Hawk Mountain the giant raises a shin, and the line of flight is narrowed. The Lookout, a bare outcropping of tumbled boulders, juts high above the narrowest part of the ridge, "like the prow of a ship," and a more effective bottleneck for migrating birds would be difficult to find. Beyond the Sanctuary to the south, the ridge zigzags and broadens, and the flight again spreads out.

As the hawks come down the ridge and pass our vantage point, alternately coasting and flapping, or circling a moment above the trees, we are keenly aware of the novelty of studying these birds from an exceedingly advantageous position. The average student in the field is obliged to look *up* to make identifications; at Hawk Mountain he frequently looks *down* upon the birds, or sees them come head-on, sometimes at eye level. It is this advantage, gained from the peculiar topography of the ridge, that reminds us constantly of a time when Hawk Mountain was once a veritable death-trap for migrating birds, when all the magnificent hawks were used as targets, and death and destruction lay like a blight over the beautiful wilderness scene.

Another main route of aerial traffic taken by the northeastern hawks is the somewhat devious coastal route, with concentration areas at Cape May, New Jersey (about 140 miles to the southeast of Hawk Mountain), and in Virginia.

The coastal flights are totally unlike our ridge migrations, which feature *Buteos* (the large, soaring hawks). At Cape May the flights begin and end much earlier than do ours, and they are made up of great numbers of *Accipiters* (sharp-shinned and Cooper's hawks), falcons, ospreys and turkey vultures, all of which (with the exception of the sharp-shinned hawk) occur in negligible numbers along the interior ridges. Appreciable flights of hawks occur on certain days along the parallel ridges to the north and west of the Kittatinny Ridge.

(You may wonder why no mention has been made of a spring migration at Hawk Mountain. We have observed a few movements of hawks in the spring, but nothing notable or comparable to the autumn flights. The northward migrating hawks seem to move quickly and over a broad front).

Our heaviest hawk flights are generally preceded by meteorological disturbances in the northern Appalachian regions. Low-pressure areas advancing across these regions appear to start the hawks off, and then, two or three days later, unless shifting winds, local rains or calms have intervened, we can be certain to see exciting and varied numbers of birds of prey. *This is the one and only predictable thing about the hawk migrations.* To illustrate, on September 15, 1935, a pronounced low-pressure area extended over northern New York and New England. Two days later we recorded 3,293 hawks of nine species.

In the fall of 1942, with the help of Ben Goodwin and Carl Siebecker, I obtained flight-speed records of 152 hawks over a measured course, using a telephone, a stop-watch and an anemometer. We found that the average rate of speed of the migrating hawks (all species considered collectively) is thirty miles per hour. Many did forty, and some nearly sixty miles per hour. Assuming an average of six hours of flight, the birds easily cover about 200 miles in a day—just about the time and mileage required for the above super-flight to register at Hawk Mountain.

There is a more or less continuous day-by-day movement of southbound hawks, even when the northern Appalachian regions are blessed with very mild autumns; the birds simply follow the impulse to migrate. But it is a diffused movement, the birds spreading out over the countryside. Drifting down from the north continuously, the hawks eventually strike up against the ridges. The birds will stick to the ridges if the invisible roller coaster of air currents is working.

When the lack of strong winds along our flyway causes the legions of hawks to drift over the open country, I receive reports from sharp-eyed observers who spot the birds in unexpected places. Thus on September 22, 1939, a calm day that brought only 19 hawks to the Sanctuary, Ira J. Weigley saw more than 500 broad-wings over Bernhardt's Valley, near Reading, a few miles to our south. On November 1, 1947, another poor day at the Sanctuary, Francis L. Newman saw more than 400 red-tails and 4 golden eagles passing over his home in West Chester, about 50 miles to the south. And on another of our dull days in 1936, Mrs. Everett S. Griscom saw "several hundred" red-tails migrating over Philadelphia, while she sat in a dentist's chair!

So we see that our hawk flights (and our widely fluctuating seasonal totals) are the substance of the immaterial winds. It is impossible, then, for us to judge whether the tribes of hawks are increasing or decreasing. We can only hope that the population curve is up. Sometimes I marvel that there are any hawks at all—they have been slaughtered so mercilessly for so long. In spite of the excellent reputations most hawks have earned for themselves, and in spite of the ever-increasing numbers of enlightened and sympathetic people, the hawks will always be at the mercy of irresponsible, trigger-happy ignoramuses. The forces of destruction are legion

SPECIES	1934	1935	1936	1937	1938	1939	1940	1941	1942	1946	1947	1948
Turkey vulture	166	374	87	44	60	146	150	182	83	64	268	300
Goshawk	123	293	177	49	9	26	11	21	9	32	5	14
Sharp-shinned hawk	1913	4237	4486	4817	3113	8529	2407	3909	3203	2409	1745	1651
Cooper's hawk	333	553	474	492	204	590	166	416	292	221	122	203
Red-tailed hawk	5609	4024	3177	4978	2230	6496	4725	4700	2378	2358	1677	2499
Red-shouldered hawk	90	181	153	163	143	314	149	198	120	248	245	268
Broad-winged hawk	2026	5459	7509	4500	10,761	5736	3159	5170	4362	3280	7791	15,454
Rough-legged hawk	20	9	9	4	—	8	4	2	—	—	—	10
Golden eagle	39	66	54	73	31	83	72	55	35	69	34	40
Bald eagle	52	67	70	38	37	64	38	50	71	42	92	88
Marsh hawk	105	153	149	160	189	273	161	254	107	171	176	186
Osprey	31	169	205	201	124	174	91	201	213	191	297	170
Peregrine falcon	25	14	36	41	24	38	25	44	36	26	19	33
Pigeon hawk	19	20	34	10	12	43	11	35	17	20	10	19
Sparrow hawk	13	123	102	141	87	184	60	196	113	98	121	142
Unidentified	208	23	11	8	—	—	7	38	38	62	52	96
TOTALS	10,772*	15,765	16,733	15,719	17,024	22,704	11,236	15,471	11,077	9,291	12,654	21,173

*September count not included.

SPECIES	TOTALS	Percent of totals	August	September	October	November
Broad-winged hawk	75,207	41.86				
Red-tailed hawk	44,851	24.96				
Sharp-shinned hawk	42,419	23.61				
Cooper's hawk	4,066	2.26				
Red-shouldered hawk	2,272	1.26				
Marsh hawk	2,084	1.16				
Osprey	2,067	1.15				
Turkey vulture	1,924	1.07				
Sparrow hawk	1,380	0.77				
Goshawk	770	0.42				
Bald eagle	709	0.38				
Golden eagle	651	0.36				
Peregrine falcon	354	0.19				
Pigeon hawk	250	0.13				
Rough-legged hawk	66	0.03				

THE GENERAL PATTERN of the hawk migrations at Hawk Mountain, showing the flight duration and abundance of each of the 15 species of hawks, based on the observations of twelve seasons: 1934-1942, 1946-1948.

and ready at all times to erase all large birds from the
heavens.

As each passing week brings subtle seasonal changes in the
far-spread landscape, so there is a corresponding change in
the character and composition of the hawk flights. In September and October, I mount to the Lookout about 7:30
A.M. (Eastern Standard Time). Within a half hour the first
hawks drift casually by the Lookout. In September the day's
flight is usually over by 4 P.M., but on days of especially heavy
flights the larger birds, such as bald eagles and ospreys, will invariably appear until dusk closes in.

A curious aspect of the September flights is the arrival,
generally, of the bulk of a day's migrants during the forenoon. Another interesting feature of the flights is the noonday lull that occurs regularly throughout the first two
months. The skies become void of hawks, which stop to feed
and to rest, presumably; but I have rarely seen the birds take
their "nooning" in the Sanctuary. In late October and November, notable numbers of hawks appear in the afternoons
as well as during the forenoons, and on many days in October I have kept a lonely vigil until the last migrants passed
aslant the setting sun. Then I have often seen them settle
down for the night within the Sanctuary. And often, the
following morning, my eighteen-power binocular has picked
out a lone sentinel on some lofty perch in the vicinity of the
Lookout, where it greeted the rising sun. In November, as
the season wanes, the duration of a day's flight is brief; generally from 9:30 or 10 A.M. until 2:30 P.M., never earlier, and
rarely later.

Late August brings the vanguard—bald eagles and ospreys
in majestic flight on their way to Florida and the Gulf Coast.
Good hawking may get under way as early as August 20th.
On that date in 1946, Jeremy Sweeton and I saw thirteen

adult bald eagles, three ospreys and ten other hawks during two thrilling afternoon hours at the Lookout; and heavens only knows what passed the rest of that windy day. The second week in September is never very eventful. But the third week is the most exciting period of the entire season, for then there is an immense and often sudden exodus of broad-wings from the North, and these birds may be a-wing along our flyway in fabulous numbers. The buoyant little broad-wings make the longest journey of any of the hawk tribe, their winter territory extending from South Mexico to Peru. Ospreys, too, are conspicuous during this week, and there is usually one day (about the 20th) when they steal the show. The broad-wings are definitely out of the picture by October 7th, and their places are taken by many sharp-shins and a smaller number of Cooper's hawks, most of which are bound for the Gulf States. From the mellow days of mid-October to mid-November, when bleak winds and snow sweep out of the north, red-tails and a surprising number of golden eagles hold the stage in the drama of migration at the Sanctuary. It is in this period that the fortunate observer at the Lookout may see as many as twelve to fourteen species of hawks, hundreds of waterfowl and throngs of small birds, all in a few hours. If, during the first week in November, boisterous winds roar frenziedly about the Lookout, we are certain to enjoy rare sport; it is the time of big hawks, when the majority of golden eagles and goshawks and red-tails spread their wings over the Sanctuary. By late November the migrations are over. An occasional golden eagle and a few red-tails, however, straggle along well into December.

As the last birds make their triumphant exodus from the stage I am often filled with mingled feelings of sadness and elation. Across the faded folds of the mountain spread deepening shadows that emphasize the retreating season. The long look across brings with it a rush of memories. I recall nostalgically the endlessly changing moods of the mountain. Gone are the greenery and the hanging mists of September; gone is the magical golden cloak that spells October; and gone now are all the birds and all our friends who have derived intense enjoyment and inspiration from the phenomena of the seasonal pageant of hawks. Perhaps it was a red-tail, in late November, of which John Burroughs wrote: "Yonder hawk, sailing peacefully away till he is lost in the horizon, is a symbol of the closing season and the departing birds."

TURKEY VULTURE

It is always pleasant to watch these great dark birds as they lazily, gracefully tack back and forth along our ridge, demonstrating their effortless conquest of the air currents. They are with us daily much of the season. But I have long since given up counting "buzzards" in September, for we have a local population of eleven or twelve pairs, and it would not do to swell our counts with the "local yokels" as I have come to call—affectionately, mind you—our resident birds.

Turkey vultures that I am reasonably confident to be outsiders appear some seasons in late September, at which time they show definite migratory behavior, as in the late afternoon of September 28, 1941, when a squadron of 52 of the birds appeared high over the "kettle," spiraling and soaring, in the manner of broad-wings, before moving south in a stately procession. A few vultures, probably migrants, show up on good flight days through October and early November. On very few occasions have we seen noteworthy flights: a compact fleet of 145 on November 5, 1935; about 180 on October 17, 1947; and upwards of 300 on November 6, 1948.

GOSHAWK

It is always a pulse-quickening event when one of these fierce corsairs of the skyways sweeps boldly into view at the Lookout; and there have been exactly 770 such events to lend zest to my 7,200 hours of observation! Several times when I have been alone—and motionless—at the Lookout, goshawks have flashed so close I could see the fire in their eyes. And once I was startled by a mighty *swish* of wings that sent a rush of air down my neck. Turning quickly, I saw an enormous goshawk, equally startled, pulling away. I had been concealed behind a rock-shelf, with only my hatless pate exposed, and probably the bird had taken my mop of hair for some mammal. It was fortunate for me that the bird had a sudden change of mind. That was the nearest I have ever come to being "crowned"—and by golden knuckles at that!

Talk to any of the hunters who frequent the few vantage points in the mountains where hawk-shooting persists, and you learn that every large hawk that passes is a *"gosh-hawk,"* to be killed if at all possible. I doubt that there is one hunter in a hundred who could correctly identify a goshawk. Many an experienced ornithologist at the Sanctuary has hesitated to name every goshawk that passes. And I frankly admit that of all the hawks, this species is the one that most often gives me trouble. I never count the bird unless I plainly see the white stripe over the eye. In any event, this wonderful, spirited bird is among the rarest of the *Raptores* along our ridge, as it is elsewhere south of the Canadian border.

Goshawk "invasions" in Pennsylvania during the seasons of 1934, 1935 and 1936 are reflected in our counts. The greatest number of goshawks that I have observed in any month was 254 during 19 days of November, 1935; heavy flights in that month occurred as follows: 32 birds on the

23rd, 51 on the 24th, and 21 on the 25th. Nothing comparable has since occurred, except possibly during the war years when daily observations were not made. Our total of 177 goshawks for 1936 seems inconsequential when compared with the 537 goshawks that were received for the five-dollar bounty during the month of November alone by the Pennylvania Game Commission. It is not hard to imagine the great numbers of harmless and beneficial hawks that must have been destroyed in Pennsylvania that year, in the hope that they would prove to be goshawks.

SHARP-SHINNED HAWK

It is a crisp day in mid-October. "Sharpies" are coursing through the treetops below us, or darting over the Lookout, affording us top views, bottom views, side views, with every feather visible. The little sharp-shin is rather easily identified, even at a distance, by its *flap, flap, flap–s–a–i–l,* and its square-tipped tail. One must be alert not to miss any, for they are plunging by every few minutes, on half-closed wings or soaring on the updrafts. A sharp-shin makes a sudden dive, landing almost atop an unsuspecting flicker. The flicker sets up a squeal that echoes through the mountain, but is off in an instant. Pursuer and pursued start a dizzy, zigzag chase through the treetops. This little drama lasts but twenty seconds, and there is no tragedy—just an oft-repeated happening, one of the numerous thrills enjoyed by the watchers. The flicker returns to its post, perhaps puffed with self-satisfaction; at any rate the better for its chase.

Of all the hawks, this little *Accipiter* is the most difficult to count by virtue of its small size and swift, erratic flight. When Hawk Mountain was a shooting paradise these were the birds that tested the gunners' skill and provided the most exciting "sport." The sharp-shins appear momentarily, darting through the trees in pursuit of small birds, or skimming over the Lookout rocks, fairly flying into our faces, and in a flash they are gone. On heavy flight days they may be seen moving rapidly at all elevations, sometimes so high (and out over the valleys) that many must escape observation.

The sharp-shin has the longest and most continuous migration of any of the hawks. They arrive in small numbers in late August, and they increase notably the last week in September. Nearly all of the first-comers are birds of the year. One curious exception stands out: on September 22, 1935, every one of 87 sharp-shins was an adult! The majority of the September sharp-shins *always* come during the afternoon. At Cape May they fly largely in the morning! Early October brings a gradual transition from immature to adult birds, and after mid-October immatures are seen infrequently. It is far from easy to differentiate ages when sharp-shins are moving in large numbers. In 1935 and 1936, however, I took great pains to obtain such data and discovered that during the former season exactly fifty per cent of the migrants were immatures, while in 1936 only twelve per cent were immatures.

Our flight-speed data on 37 "sharpies" ranged from 16 m.p.h. to 60 m.p.h.. A sharp-shin *gliding* on updrafts created by a northwest wind of 20-mile velocity, was literally "going like 60!" The *air-speed* of another sharp-shin, flapping continuously, was 34 m.p.h.

Record "sharpie" days have occurred as follows: 1935—512 on October 2, and 680 on October 4; 1936—901 on October 19; 1937—900 on October 7, and 734 on October 8; 1939—1,658 on October 7; 1942—627 on October 19.

COOPER'S HAWK

Closely paralleling the sharp-shin migration—though on a much smaller scale—is the migration of the Cooper's hawk. As with the sharp-shin, the immatures precede the adults, and the latter make up the majority of the migrants. October brings the greatest numbers, with 20 to 50 (rarely 75) on a good flight day. A record number of 127 was obtained on October 8, 1937; and the next best record is that of 91 birds on October 14, 1939.

The proportion of Cooper's to sharp-shins is roughly 10 per cent, the same figure that holds at Cape May. Twelve flight-speed records range from 21 m.p.h. to 55 m.p.h., with an average speed of 29.3 m.p.h.

RED-TAILED HAWK

After the excitement of the broad-wing migration it is pleasant to anticipate the glorious days when red-tails dominate the skyway parade. The red-tail flights, though entirely unlike those of the fabulous broad-wings, are quite as spectacular.

My memory often conjures up days when the wind shrieks out of a storm-cleared sky and the Lookout may wear its first light mantle of snow; then it is that the big red-tails converge along our flyway and put on their own special show. They advance across the turbulent aerial currents with hardly a quiver of their broad, confident wings; they come singly, or in pairs, but there may be caravans of twenty to thirty, sometimes forty birds, extending to the farthermost folds of the ridge. They disappear quickly, for their traveling speed averages almost thirty miles an hour. Now and then, one mounts high in the sky, soaring in ever-widening spirals, a red tail flashing in the sunlight, until, having gained sufficient altitude, it is soon a mote in the blue. On such a day, if we brave the chill blasts until deep shadows have enveloped the mountain and the last bird heralds the first glow of eventide, we may run up a score of 400 to 800 of these impressive *Buteos*.

Although a few red-tails appear over the Sanctuary during the first weeks of the season, their migration never gets under way before mid-October. Indeed, the major flights generally occur the last days of October and during early November.

The red-tail flight is composed predominantly of adults. Age determinations are difficult to make, due to the many days when the birds fly too high, or too far out from the ridge. A composite check of 16,620 red-tails that I was able to study during seven seasons showed 1,782 (12 per cent) to be birds-of-the-year.

A poor showing of red-tails at the Sanctuary during some autumns may be attributed to excessively mild weather. Strong northerly winds are a prerequisite to concentrated ridge flights, in the case of this species. Ideal flight conditions for red-tails prevailed in 1939; hence our total of 6,496 for that season. Our most remarkable single flight of this species was of 1,144 birds, on October 24, 1939; the next best passage, of 987 red-tails, occurred on October 31, 1937.

As is well known, the red-tailed hawk displays wide variation of plumage. At Hawk Mountain I have seen these birds in all gradations, from melanistic phases to birds with creamy underparts, no trace of abdominal bands and very pale heads. In addition, I have records of eight albinos—5 of them "as white as the driven snow."

Most of the hawk species progress along the ridge in absolute silence. Not so the red-tails, which often advertise their presence near the Lookout with their characteristic squealing **whistle**.

RED-SHOULDERED HAWK

It has always been a source of wonder to me that these handsome *Buteos* are so few, so poorly represented in our ridge flights. Why should this bird, so like its broad-winged and red-tailed relatives (which together make up 67 per cent of the flights), be so scarce along our flyway?

Observers at the Lookout need not be confused by immatures of this species and of broad-wings. The latter are generally well on their way through Mexico when the red-shoulders enter the scene, although we have a handful of records of September red-shoulders.

Our red-shoulders are largely adults. They come regularly, but in very small numbers, from mid-October until the end of the season. We may see ten to twenty birds on good flight days in the third week of October. Five times only in the whole range of my experience have I seen thirty or more red-shoulders in one day; such occurrences are concurrent with good red-tail flights. Our best red-shoulder flight was of 60 birds on October 24, 1948. The day previous mist-laden southeast winds lowered the curtain on the show at the Sanctuary. I led a party of observers from Rochester, New York, to Ontelaunee Reservoir, a few miles to the south, to see waterfowl. To our surprise, we saw 17 red-shoulders move one by one along the crest of a low hill at the reservoir; and all the birds went over in a very few minutes, toward the southwest. Perhaps these birds (and many more) might have passed the Lookout had the winds been northerly. The observation points up how many hawks we must miss on southeast winds. Or does it provide us with a clue to the relative scarcity of the red-shoulder along our ridge?

BROAD-WINGED HAWK

Seventy-five thousand broad-wings counted and *protected* in twelve Septembers is a record of which we are very proud! But imagine what a Lenape Indian might have seen from our Lookout rocks, on September 17, 1734, before the gun, the axe, the plow had opened up the continent. My guess is that he must have seen far more broad-wings on that one day than we now see during an entire season. And what will the bird student of the year 2049 see from our vantage points? By the grace of God and the best use of man's wisdom, we hope that his September skies will blossom forth with the miracle of the gentle broad-wings. We are doing our best to make that possible!

Soon after the middle of August a few young broad-wings start off on the first lap of the long journey to their tropical wintering grounds. Late that month many more travelers are awing. On August 31, 1947, we counted 67 broad-wings; and an identical count was made exactly a year later! As more and more broad-wings, young and old, stretch their wings toward the south, we pray that favorable winds will prevail from September 16th to 20th. There will be at least one day in that period when phenomenal numbers of these little *Buteos* literally pour across our airways. Several hundred broad-wings may appear any day at the Sanctuary until late September; then the flight ends abruptly. A few stragglers show up until October 7th, and I have records of two belated birds, both adults: October 22, 1941, and November 1, 1946.

The number of broad-wings that we do *not* see over Hawk Mountain must be considerable! Sometimes when there is no wind and the flight conditions seem to be unfavorable, the birds may come en masse, but so high that it is sheer luck to spot them. At such times these hawks may use thermals, or they may simply follow the line of the ridge. Examples of flights that could easily have gone unrecorded may be of interest. September 16, 1935: between 10:15 A.M. and 11:15 A.M. I saw a continuous movement of broad-wings directly over the ridge, but so high as to be almost invisible to the unaided eye; I counted 703 birds. September 16, 1942: a surprising flight of 607 broad-wings, passing on both sides of the ridge, some far to the south and many very high; at 11:45 A.M. I counted 220 so high that they were visible only with the aid of my 8-power binocular. September 13, 1948: a still, hot day, and only 347 high-flying hawks. But twenty miles down the ridge, near Bethel, Theodore Hake spotted 711 broad-wings traveling at an extreme height.

We have "timed" broad-wings traveling with a southeast wind of ten miles velocity, at 30 and 32 m.p.h. One bird attained 40 m.p.h. on a southeast wind of fifteen miles velocity.

Although the broad-wing has the most restricted migration period of any of the *Raptores,* it nevertheless enjoys supremacy of numbers. In "Red-letter Days" I have tried to convey some idea of the impressive flights of broad-wings at Hawk Mountain.

ROUGH-LEGGED HAWK

To the rough-leg belongs the distinction of being the rarest hawk at Hawk Mountain—excepting, of course, the accidental occurrences of gyrfalcons. Four entire seasons passed without the appearance of a single bird. Our earliest record is that of a bird on October 6, 1935, but most of the sixty-six occurrences have been in late October and in November.

GOLDEN EAGLE

Formerly considered a very rare bird in the East, our intensive observations have proved that this species is a regular transient along the Kittatinny Ridge. Golden eagles are a great attraction at the Sanctuary. We look for the majority of them during the last half of the season, and well into December. Thirty records obtain for September, however. Our earliest record is that of an immature, on September 2, 1947. It is not at all unusual for us to see seven or eight individuals in one day; and once, on November 5, 1946, a group of bird watchers had the thrill of their ornithological lives when they saw thirteen of these splendid birds. During the first six seasons, immatures averaged fifty per cent of the total; but I regret to report a steady decline. The second period of six seasons shows a drop to twenty-five per cent, and in 1948 only one immature golden eagle was observed.

It is impossible, in a mere paragraph, to do justice to these lordly birds, whose origins and destinations have been shrouded in mystery. The golden eagles of Hawk Mountain, therefore, merit a chapter to themselves.

BALD EAGLE

Our national birds are the curtain-raisers of the hawking season. Any windy afternoon, from mid-August until the flood-tide of broad-wings has passed, we may see impressive numbers of bald eagles sailing majestically over the Sanctuary. While other hawks have been raising families, our bald eagles have enjoyed freedom from all care and responsibility. But now *their* season of procreation is almost at hand. So they are Florida-bound, to raise families, and to await Charles Broley, the "eagle man." Broley, the retired Canadian banker, indulges a unique and dangerous wintertime hobby: climbing to eagles' nests to band the young birds— and he has more than a thousand eaglet bandings to his credit. Broley's birds have been recovered, in the summer months, as far north as the Canadian Provinces, near Hudson's Bay, and in central Manitoba.

We seldom see these magnificent birds before mid-morning. I believe that they take their time to test their wings on the morning currents, preferring to "loafe and invite their souls" wherever they have happened to settle down the evening before. Anyway, most of our eagles come in the afternoon, sometimes after all the other hawks have passed. Because of their habit of migrating very late in the day, I am certain that we miss some of the birds. Although the bald eagle migrations extend through the entire season, 82 per cent (583) of the birds have been observed before the end of September. I have 79 records of October visitants, and 47 records for November and December.

The grandest eagle show it has been our privilege to enjoy took place on September 6, 1935. John Treadway and I sat spellbound as we watched one after another of 33 bald eagles (all but six of them adults). They appeared as motes on the horizon, and then in a matter of seconds they were directly above us, soaring and circling on rigid, ebony wings. One of the birds let out a soft whistling note, quite musical, which I have never again heard. Fifty-four other hawks of six species (mainly ospreys) were the lesser figures that moved across the deep blue sky that exceedingly windy *afternoon*. The last eagle sailed from view at 5:48 P.M.

It is not at all unusual for us to see ten to eighteen bald eagles in a few hours, in the early part of the season. Another flight I shall not soon forget occurred during the afternoon of August 29, 1948, the fourth day of a terrific heat wave that left most Easterners stupefied. The temperature was

94° on the north slope of the Lookout. But a brisk northwest wind activated 79 hawks to exercise their pinions, and of these 10 were adult bald eagles.

Immature birds have averaged 59 per cent of the bald eagles that were counted from 1934 to 1939. In recent years, however, there has been a sharp decline of immatures to 37 per cent—a circumstance that closely parallels our data on immature golden eagles.

MARSH HAWK

Although the graceful "harrier" plays a very minor role in the pageant of our hawk migrations, it nevertheless is a bird of considerable interest. It is featured in our counts almost daily, and throughout the period of migration. Marsh hawks often appear coursing low along either side of the ridge, quite indifferent to the air currents. Many drift in from the north, cross the ridge at right angles to the regular line of flight, then continue south over the broad hump of the mountain. October brings the majority of the marsh hawks. The largest number I have counted in one day was eighteen, on November 2, 1946.

An interesting and undeviating flight sequence has been observed each season: immatures make up nearly all of the August and September migrants; both sexes as well as immatures come in varying numbers during October, while late in the migration the males outnumber the others. During four seasons the ratio of immatures to adults varied from 33.9 per cent to 48.3 per cent. But in 1942 the ratio of immatures to adults was 77 per cent.

OSPREY

People making their first visit to the Sanctuary are often amazed to see ospreys in passage over the rugged crests of our mountain. It does seem unnatural to see the "fish hawk" so far removed from the seacoast or large inland bodies of water. Nevertheless, the gull-like flight of the osprey thrills us almost daily from about August 20th until late September. An "osprey day" is an annual event, occurring on or about the twentieth of September, and at least 40 of the big birds may be counted.

In 1947 the ospreys gave us a double-feature performance. They provided Mrs. Edge with a special show, on the usual date—September 20th. It was a cold, disagreeable day, and sheets of dripping fog, driving in from the southeast, veiled the Lookout much of the time. The prospects for hawking appeared to be nil. Some 30 visitors braved the impending rain to tarry at the Lookout, hoping to see a few birds. During the midafternoon, Mrs. Edge and I sat comfortably in my car, at the entrance, excitedly watching ospreys materialize out of the mists, sometimes four or six birds at once, all quite low, and winging toward the southwest. Most of the fifty-eight ospreys that we counted were not seen by the people at the Lookout. But that fine show was surpassed only two days later.

It had rained hard all morning. Clearing noonday skies and roaring winds from the northwest presaged a rare and exciting afternoon. The only observers on hand were Albert and Eva Schnitzer, of Elizabeth, N. J. We began to see hawks immediately upon our arrival at the Lookout, at 1:10 P.M. Every bird seemed to be in a frightful hurry to clear the ridge, and ospreys in particular seemed "hell-bent for election." One osprey took time out to make three power-dives at a golden eagle, the latter taking the performance good-naturedly. We stuck out the watch till sunset—a truly beautiful one—and watched the last osprey, at 5:50 P.M., wind up an unprecedented flight for that species. The box score for the afternoon was 19 sharp-shins, 1 Cooper's, 204 broadwings, 2 red-tails, 15 bald eagles, 2 golden eagles, *78 ospreys,* 2 marsh and 2 sparrow hawks. It was the Schnitzers' first visit to the Sanctuary; beginners' luck!

Ospreys occur sporadically in October, and we have two November records: a bird seen on the 14th, in 1935; another on the 6th, in 1937.

Our flight-speed records of 16 ospreys range from 20 to 80 m.p.h. A few birds, traveling with a southeast wind of 15 mile velocity, made 36 to 48 m.p.h. An osprey sailing along the ridge at 80 m.p.h. was evidently making use of a very strong thermal, so that the bird was in reality in steep diving flight without losing altitude.

GYRFALCON

What are the chances of seeing a gyrfalcon at Hawk Mountain? The answer to this sixty-four-dollar question, according to my best judgment, is about one in sixty thousand. After all, the gyrfalcon, a bird of the Arctic wastes, is an accidental winter visitant, and it is hardly to be expected this far south.

Recent studies of the gyrfalcon indicate that there is but one species in North America, and that the various black, white and gray plumages are only color phases. My experience with gyrfalcons before coming to Hawk Mountain had been nil. Even now I cannot say that I am on speaking terms with the bird! I have 6 gyrfalcon records for the mountain, but I prefer to consign 3 of these records to the hypothetical list.

A gyrfalcon in very dark plumage occurred in a flight of

369 hawks (of 13 species) on October 12, 1934. The bird spent two minutes swooping round the Lookout, plunging at passing sharp-shins and red-tails, to the amazement and delight of Mrs. Edge, Mrs. Alfred Edey and myself.

Three weeks later I had the rare good luck to see another gyrfalcon. This time a bird in white plumage passed the Lookout very low, and leisurely, late in the afternoon of November 2nd. It was a perfect climax to a red-letter day which produced 1,013 hawks—and a raven just to counterbalance the great white visitor.

The circumstances attending the visit of the third gyrfalcon were quite dramatic. I held a lonely watch on the morning of October 16, 1936. Low-hanging clouds and heavy mists curtained the terrain. Not a hawk had come. After a time a large flock of wild geese swept out of the mists, and their clarion notes, resounding through the mountain, seemed to convey tidings of something wonderful about to happen. The mists presently scattered, and at 11:20 A.M. a huge falcon, in very dark plumage, pulled up its sails almost directly above me, and within seventy feet. It veered a trifle, hesitated, and then sailed off towards the south, moving very slowly; a gyrfalcon indubitably.

Our gyrfalcon records are by no means unique. Doctor Witmer Stone has reported a dark-colored gyrfalcon killed by a farmer on January 7, 1927, near Manheim, Lancaster County (about twenty miles below the Kittatinny Ridge). A specimen of the white-phase gyrfalcon in the Reading Public Museum was killed along our ridge, twenty miles above the Sanctuary, on November 11, 1928. And Earl L. Poole, Curator of the Reading Museum, saw a light gray individual at Lake Ontelaunee, a few miles south of the Sanctuary, on October 28, 1941. Records of gyrfalcons for the New York City area extend from early October to late April.

PEREGRINE FALCON

The picturesque peregrine, or duck hawk, plays an insignificant role in the great hawk flights of our flyway. Because it is rare, because it is a genius of power, and a bird personality whose praises have been sung by countless generations of men, the vision of a peregrine flashing down our ridge is always attended by spontaneous, enthusiastic applause from observers. We usually have no more than a fleeting glimpse of the peregrine; its motto as it zips past the observers is "full speed ahead."

At Hawk Mountain the peregrine may be seen at any time during the entire season. Single birds are the general rule. You can imagine our excitement, therefore, when we tallied 8 peregrines on October 12, 1936; 11 on October 7, 1937; 7 on September 23, 1938; and 7 on October 8, 1941. These are trifling figures, to be sure, when contrasted with those of Cape May where, at the height of the falcon flight, as many as 25 peregrines may be counted in *one day!* Our 354 peregrine occurrences have been distributed as follows: September, 97; October, 232; November, 25.

Rarely have we observed any hawks capturing prey on Hawk Mountain, but one Sunday afternoon in 1941 we saw an immature duck hawk streaking along the north slope of the ridge. A few passerine birds were flying at right angles to the falcon's headlong flight. As we watched, one of the small birds was suddenly intercepted by the peregrine, which, without veering from its course, struck and grabbed it. The peregrine then wove back and forth over the ridge with the bird in its talons—a beautiful and amazing flight—dropping and retrieving its prey. So far as we could see, the small bird was consumed while the falcon was awing.

Again, one day in early September, 1948, a peregrine put

on a breath-taking act for the benefit of a dozen spellbound spectators. The bird was first sighted at least two miles up the ridge, and high above the south slope, where it circled, flapped, and glided. Only after much study did I realize that it was a peregrine. Then the bird made a swoop—a long slant, straight and arrowy—to its mark: a medium-sized bird winging toward us, on the *north* side of the Lookout. The hawk seized the bird as easily as you would pluck a daisy, then flew quickly eastwards with its feebly fluttering prey. It all happened in a matter of seconds. When the feathered torpedo made its plunge, the victim was easily one and a half miles away!

PIGEON HAWK

This little falcon (I am among those who prefer the name merlin) ranks second in point of rarity along our flyway, but it is, I think, the rarest *Raptore* that occurs normally in the State of Pennsylvania. My earliest record, September 10, 1935; and the latest, November 17, 1939. Single birds are the rule, although we have known days (usually in mid-October) when as many as six or eight have occurred, with flights of sparrow hawks. And on one outstanding day, October 8, 1941, fourteen merlins appeared in a flight of 436 hawks of twelve species (which included seven peregrines). On this same day, "hundreds" of these falcons were reported at Cape May, New Jersey.

Most of these hawks dash by the Lookout at speeds faster than you can say "Look—a pigeon hawk!" Reginald Hartwell, visiting the Sanctuary one week end in October, 1948, with a party of bird students representing the Genesee Ornithological Society, of Rochester, New York, has described vividly an experience with a falcon of this species: "One highlight of the morning was the exhibition given us by a pigeon hawk which swooped in over our heads and perched briefly in a tree behind us. Then he shot down over the brow of the Lookout, snatched a small bird in midair and proceeded with it to a dead stub on the ridge below, where he enjoyed a leisurely breakfast. . . . After half an hour or so, he flew into the updraft over the ridge and treated us to a most spectacular display of falcon aerobatics. Snatching up a wind-blown leaf (or butterfly, we couldn't tell which), he carried it up into the blue and let it go in the high wind. Then he dived after it in a magnificent, mile-long stoop, caught it deftly and flew up again to repeat the process all over again several times before leaving us."

SPARROW HAWK

The diminutive but valiant sparrow hawks are among the cohorts of the early-moving bald eagles and ospreys. From time to time one of these engaging mites of hawkdom may be seen loitering above the ridge, plunging at passing *Buteos* and other hawks. Several times I have seen them beset eagles, but the sky-born dignitaries never seem to be troubled by the falconine atoms of impudence.

A glance at the totals shows that twice as many of these little falcons use our flyway as do peregrines and merlins combined. Most of our sparrow hawks come in September; their numbers diminish during October, and I have but six records for November. Fewer than six sparrow hawks ordinarily show up in one day, but on good flight days we may see ten to thirty individuals. The best record is of thirty-eight birds on September 26, 1937. About 65 per cent of our sparrow hawks are males.

CHAPTER 13 — RED-LETTER DAYS

Each season brings its special crop of memory-rich days. Such days do not necessarily call for a sky full of hawks. My lonely vigil of October 16, 1936, produced but one hawk—a black gyrfalcons; none will deny that that was an extra-special day! Great, glistening wedges of swans flowing across the azure bowl of the sky—otherwise devoid of birds—have been as soul-moving as anything I have experienced at Hawk Mountain. Then, too, there are those days of inexpressible loveliness, usually after a storm, when the mists and the clouds, the play of shadows and sunshine, create a kaleidoscopic profusion of mountain moods that hold us spellbound; and such days can be more stirring than a mighty symphony. The unexpected arrival at the Lookout of some cherished friend can stamp that day as outstanding! And I shall never forget the bleak November day that one little snow bunting and I (to paraphrase Celia Thaxter) shared the Lookout rocks. All these, and more, spell red-letter days to me.

But suppose we narrow down our designation to cover only those days when hawks flood the Sanctuary skyways, as though in fulfillment of a hawk-lover's hopes and dreams. Such days come at least once each season, no matter how poor that season may be. A miracle day often takes place during the third week in September; then legions of broad-wings sweep down from the North, like a wave of crusading banners. In recent years bird students have flocked to the Sanctuary to camp that entire week, in order to be on hand for the hoped for *big day*. Only in this way can the ardent bird watcher be assured of witnessing a superlative flight and enjoying the ornithological "thrill of a lifetime." Another promising, though less dependable period, is early November. This is my choice, though the weather be rigorous, because of the added spice and excitement that comes with large and varied numbers of waterfowl which we may see.

So, gleaning from my notebooks a few representative "redletter days," we shall see some of the promised hosts of hawks pass quickly in review. But mere words cannot recapture the delight, the exaltation and the inspiration that the birds have passed on to us.

Friday, November 2, 1934

A raw, biting wind from the northwest produced the choicest list to date. I shivered at the Lookout from 8 A.M. to 5 P.M. The busiest hours were from 9 to 11, 12 to 1, and 2 to 4; and how the birds streaked by! Red-tails in the main, flying at varying levels, very low during the early and late part of the day, often extremely high during midday.

The grand climax to the flight came at 4:20 P.M. when a white gyrfalcon sailed by and disappeared into the pinktinged clouds. The last batch of red-tails was passing. I was chilled to the bone, ready to leave, when the great white bird appeared, flying slowly, some two hundred feet out and well below the rocks, so that I looked down upon it. The bird was almost pure white and larger than a red-tail, which followed closely.

Scarcely a half hour before the gyrfalcon came, a raven sailed along. Two wonder-birds in one day—and no witnesses! The day's count of 1,013 hawks included: 1 vulture,

2 goshawks, 129 sharp-shins, 8 Cooper's, 853 red-tails, 13 red-shoulders, 6 marsh and the gyrfalcon.

Tuesday, September 17, 1935

A clear day, with light to moderate southeasterly winds; 42°-66°. Very soon after my arrival [at 7:45 A.M.], flock upon flock of small *Buteos* came drifting down the south flank of the ridge. The birds flew very low during the first hour or so of observation; thereafter they were seen at varying levels, sometimes quite high. When the birds reached the "kettle" (the great bowl of the forest below the Lookout, on our right), having been strung out along the ridge, they would concentrate into swirling flocks, and then ascend gradually on the updrafts. After milling round and round, sometimes over our heads, until sufficient altitude was gained; the birds would "peel off" in long glides toward the southwest, again strung out in long lines. As many as 50 or 60 broad-wings at a time were in the air above us. Richard M. May, of Hagerstown, Maryland, arrived in the early forenoon, and gave his much-needed help in counting. The height of the migration came between 9 A.M. and 11 A.M.; it began to wane about 3:45 P.M., and a half hour later it was definitely over. Our count of 3,293 hawks included 15 vultures (local birds), 70 sharp-shins, 32 Cooper's, 4 red-tails, about 3,153 broad-wings, 2 bald eagles, 3 marsh, 13 ospreys and 1 sparrow hawk.

Of small birds, last night's sharp drop in temperature brought great numbers, mostly warblers. A summer tanager, 3 pine siskins and a red-headed woodpecker were the outstanding passerines.

Wednesday, October 2, 1935

Clear and cold, with brisk northwest winds; 35°-57°. How we enjoyed the sharp-shins skimming over the rocks and passing so close we could see them eye to eye! They came mainly after 9 o'clock, two or three birds at a time, in a steady procession that lasted until late afternoon. Irma and I were alone at the Lookout this glorious day; a pity it could not have been shared with our many friends. The choicest bird of the day was a raven. We saw it cross the ridge at noon, and twice we heard a throaty *croak*. Four hours later our raven (the same?) went over again, reversing its flight. We counted 688 hawks of twelve species: 4 vultures, 2 goshawks, 512 sharp-shins, 48 Cooper's, 17 red-tails, 14 red-shoulders, 70 broad-wings, 6 ospreys, 2 marsh, 1 peregrine, 2 pigeon and 10 sparrow hawks.

Sunday, October 6, 1935

Heavily overcast, and strong northwest winds during the afternoon only; 40° average. In spite of the raw weather, we had a fine, jolly crowd, mostly Philadelphians, and a few people from Delaware; also a lady from Paris. Some of us stayed until 5:30 P.M., when the only sunlight of the day fell briefly on the mountain, and the western sky lighted up in a great splash of crimson, gold and purple. A "hoot-owl" called from the far ridge.

Very few small birds. A flock of 12 juncos at the Lookout, unmindful of the visitors. We saw 24 "honkers" in the early afternoon; and just before sunset a long line of about 150 white-winged scoters passed swiftly toward the southeast.

Today's 14 species of hawks constitutes a record for variety. All birds were flying high and well out of gun-range: 1 vulture, 1 goshawk, 149 sharp-shins, 62 Cooper's, 193 red-tails, 33 red-shoulders, 1 rough-leg, 6 golden eagles, 1 bald eagle, 4 marsh, 11 ospreys, 2 peregrines, 4 pigeon and 3 sparrow-hawks—471 individuals.

Sunday, October 20, 1935

Clear, with moderate winds from northwest; 56°-64°. A busy and successful day. Irma directed 250 visitors up the path to the Lookout. The rocks were hardly visible, draped as they were with colorful throngs of children, Boy Scouts and grown-ups, all craning their necks skyward at the passing hawks. Everybody just as happy as could be! Only two years ago this day there could well have been 250 hunters—and two to three hundred dead hawks. Among the visitors was my old friend, Dr. John B. May, all the way from Boston, and other friends—Dr. and Mrs. Thomas B. Nolan, with two other couples, from Washington, D. C., and Mrs. Edge, as well as a score of members of the Delaware Valley Ornithological Club. A stork must have passed over the Sanctuary, for a babe-in-arms appeared at the Lookout. But the most surprising visitor was Mrs. Koch, who came late in the afternoon, creating quite a sensation; it was her first trip to the mountaintop, although she has lived within sight of it for fifty-two years.

The score for the day: 497 hawks of thirteen species—4 vultures, 4 goshawks, 243 sharp-shins, 8 Cooper's, 225 redtails, 3 red-shoulders, 1 rough-leg, 3 golden eagles, 1 osprey, 2 marsh, 1 peregrine, 1 sparrow hawk.

Monday, November 18, 1935

Mostly cloudy, very strong nothwest winds, and temperature average 28°. Yesterday's snowfall rendered the road impassable. I walked to the Lookout, from Drehersville, over trackless snow which deepened with my ascent until, near the entrance, the snow blanket lay just nine inches thick. The trees, festooned with heavy, wet snow, arched over the narrow road, almost blocking passage. I reached the Lookout at 9:20, but there was not much stirring until almost 11 o'clock. My feet were soon as cold as the rocks. The next three hours were miserable ones, but I was determined to stick to my post and see what might fly. It was well that I did, even though I almost turned into an icicle. I wouldn't have missed today's eagles drifting down the desolate arctic scene, nor the waterfowl flashing across the cloud-packed skies. Extraordinary color and scenic contrasts highlighted the day. To the north, as far as I could see, the snow blanketed all things, and leaden clouds rolled swiftly in the teeth of the young whirlwind. But in the southeast, the Great Valley presented open fields and snowless roads; great green patches of wheat glinted with darts of sunlight. When I quit my post at 4:30, some time after the last red-tail had passed, the clouds opened everywhere and the dull northern sky now turned a glorious gold, while amethyst clouds scudded across a sea-green sky. As I retraced my tracks to Drehersville, and toward the sinking sun, I discovered that many deer, and a raccoon had crossed my tracks of the morning. And so ended a day of sheer beauty and adventure. Nor could it have been more rewarding ornithologically. I saw 12 goshawks, 1 Cooper's, 152 red-tails, 6 golden eagles, 1 marsh hawk, 38 Canada geese, 3 American mergansers, 35 pintails, 1 green-winged teal, 15 black ducks, 4 horned larks and 700 rusty blackbirds.

Thursday, September 17, 1936

Overcast, threatening skies all morning, clearing after 1:30 P.M.; brisk northerly winds all day; 62°-74°. Small *Buteos* began coming at 8:15 and soon after they were coming thick and fast: I counted 280 between 10:28 and 10:35! The majority passed directly over the ridge within range of gunshot. This flight of low-flying hawks was continuous for five hours. [Picture the slaughter of the earlier days!] At 12:30 some 150 broad-wings passed well out over the valley on the north side of the ridge. Sharp-shins came in numbers after 1:30, as did ospreys and eagles. At 2:30 I scanned the zenith with my 8-power glasses, just in time to make a hasty count of 200 broad-wings dashing westwards. They were flying so high as to be scarcely visible to the unaided eye. . . . After this the birds flew at varying levels, some very low. There was a steady stream of hawks, a few groups notable as follows: 113 birds at 4 o'clock; 170 birds at 4:08; 126 birds at 4:55; 81 at 5:08; and 42 at 5:20. The last birds seen were 2 ospreys, at 5:47. The count for the day was 3,604 hawks: 1 vulture, 3 goshawks, 92 sharp-shins, 10 Cooper's, 9 red-tails, 3,400 broad-wings, 2 golden eagles, 18 bald eagles, 8 marsh, 52 ospreys, 1 pigeon and 10 sparrow hawks. There were no visitors, unfortunately, to witness this spectacular flight.

Monday, October 12, 1936

Heavily overcast during forenoon; clear rest of day; cool, brisk, northwest winds all day. Almost all of the forty-three visitors to the Lookout were real bird students, taking advantage of the holiday. It was refreshing not to be plagued with inconsequential questions! Among the visitors was the amazing John Kieran; and there was an amiable millionaire, from near Philadelphia, fraternizing with everyone. We put on the best show possible for the fine gathering. There was a heavy flight of hawks from 7:45 A.M. until 3 P.M. Of birds other than hawks, the *pièce de résistance* was a raven which flew within fifty feet of us, at 2:30 P.M., passing up the ridge to the east! We saw 100 double-crested cormorants, 13 herring gulls, 9 snow geese, 24 Canada geese, 30 pintails, 3 black ducks, 3 great blue herons. The flight of 688 hawks included: 3 goshawks, 472 sharp-shins, 76 Cooper's, 97 red-tails, 9 red-shoulders, 1 golden eagle, 4 marsh, 4 ospreys, 8 peregrines, 6 pigeon and 8 sparrow hawks.

Monday, October 19, 1936

Bright, with moderate northwest wind; 34°-55°. Yesterday I told a numbers of visitors (our register showed that 742 had climbed to the Lookout during the day, and there had been a fine flight of 602 hawks and 507 waterfowl) that if they could return today they would experience a still better flight! I reached the Lookout soon after 7 A.M. In the course of the morning, ten persons appeared who were able to follow my advice; among these was Dr. Ernst Mayr. The group had the benefit of one of the finest shows I have recorded—and certainly the second best flight of this season.

All birds were low-flying until 10:45 (425 passed, mostly sharp-shins) and many dashed over our heads. From 11 to 3 o'clock, the hawks flew at all levels, but after 3 o'clock they flew low. There was no noonday lull. The last bird, a red-tail, went by at 4:35. Had it been 1933 or earlier, there would have been a sickening slaughter. Instead, it was a day of inspiration for those of us who were privileged to be here.

Some 1,350 crows also passed down the ridge. Two flocks of wild geese went over, one of 38 birds, another of 51 birds, and this latter flock had one small goose which may well have been a Hutchin's goose. . . . The 1,516 hawks comprised 6 goshawks, 901 sharp-shins, 61 Cooper's, 519 red-tails, 6 red-shoulders, 5 golden eagles, 7 marsh, 1 osprey, 2 peregrines and 8 sparrow hawks.

Sunday, October 31, 1937

Crystal clear weather, with fresh northwest winds all day; 34°-52°. One of the most remarkable flights on record. The first hawk appeared at 7:10 A.M. We recorded 142 to 9 A.M., 307 to 10 A.M., 500 to 11, and 560 to noon. The majority flew very high and well out of range of gunshot. Red-tails were the order of the day—750 counted up to 4 P.M., and 235 coming in a steady stream from 4 P.M. to 5 P.M.

In addition to the hawks, there was plenty of "gravy" to whet the appetites of 308 observers: 1,300 crows, 85 blue-birds, 125 purple finches, hundreds of goldfinches, 25 pine siskins, 800 rusty blackbirds, 500 grackles, 200 red-wings, 1 wild turkey, 36 loons, 75 Canada geese, 1 Hutchins's goose,

12 herring gulls and 3 ring-billed gulls. The score on 1,158 hawks: 1 vulture, 3 goshawks, 131 sharp-shins, 16 Cooper's, 985 red-tails, 3 red-shoulders, 9 golden eagles, 2 bald eagles, 7 marsh and 1 peregrine.

September 22 through 26, 1938

A record broad-wing flight followed the hurricane that devastated New England. Our pluperfect hawking was preceded locally by five dreary days of continuous rain. The broad-wings, which normally migrate steadily, had been dammed up. And now that the deluge had ended, the birds lost no time in resuming their migrations.

September 22nd brought smiling blue skies and moderate westerly winds. Innumerable warblers were in evidence. The day's count of 918 hawks included 885 broad-wings of which 700 appeared between 9 A.M. and 11 A.M.

The following day, the 23rd, produced ideal flight conditions. Only 6 hawks were seen during the first hour of observation, but 825 were tallied by noon, and the total for the day was 2,062, which included in addition to 1,785 broad-wings, the following: 187 sharp-shins, 17 Cooper's, 3 red-tails, 9 bald eagles, 2 marsh, 32 ospreys, 7 peregrines, 3 pigeon and 17 sparrow hawks. The birds flew leisurely but in steady numbers, in no very large groups, without any of the customary milling, and the flight continued until 5:20 P.M.

On the third day, the memorable 24th, great numbers of passerine birds rushed past the Lookout. I estimated 100 flickers, 250 blue jays, 400 cedar waxwings, countless warblers and finches, and many chimney swifts. Only 40 hawks were seen until 9 o'clock, but thereafter they appeared in swarms: 780 between 9 and 10; 1,120 between 10 and 11; 1,260 between 11 and noon; 530 between noon and 1 P.M.; and diminishing numbers until 4 o'clock, but absolutely nothing after that hour! The heightened noonday passage of hawks was altogether contrary to our usual experience for this date. At one time as many as 436 broad-wings were seen in a compact, swirling flock. Throughout the morning the broad-wings flew very low, and in a steady stream on *both* sides of the ridge—an unusual procedure, in view of the light northerly wind which ordinarily keeps the birds on the north side of the ridge. The flight was normal during the afternoon, however. The census would have been utterly impossible had it not been for the assistance of a sharp-eyed observer who tallied every hawk that appeared on one side of the ridge. Upwards of a hundred observers witnessed at least a part of this amazing flight. The day's count follows: 13 vultures, 185 sharp-shins (nearly all after 1:30 P.M.), 18 Cooper's, 3 red-tails, 4,078 broad-wings, 4 bald eagles, 5 marsh, 9 ospreys, 1 peregrine, 1 pigeon and 8 sparrow hawks, totalling 4,325 raptors.

On the 25th (Sunday), a surprising early-morning movement of broad-wings took place. A total of 493 hawks came through between 7:30 A.M. and 9 A.M.; 287 between 9 and 10; 202 between 10 and 11; and only 381 went by the rest of the day—200 between 3:30 and 4:30. More than 500 visitors had an opportunity to witness this first-rate flight of 1,363 hawks of nine species: 130 sharp-shins, 16 Cooper's, 32 red-tails, 1,166 broad-wings, 1 bald eagle, 4 marsh, 2 ospreys, 1 peregrine and 11 sparrow hawks.

The fifth and last day of these spectacular flights was bright and warm, as were the previous days; light southerly breezes prevailed. Another huge wave of small birds appeared. All the hawks flew very high, and there was much milling about of the broad-wings. Only 18 came by from 8 to 9 o'clock, but 662 were counted during the succeeding hour, and 395 between 10 and 11. The count for the day was 1,606 hawks: 22 vultures, 70 sharp-shins, 4 Cooper's, 3 red-tails, 1,492 broad-wings, 2 bald eagles, 3 marsh, 6 ospreys and 4 sparrow hawks.

In this five-day period, 10,274 hawks were counted, and of these, 9,406 individuals, or better than nine-tenths, were broad-wings. In reporting these flights in *The Auk* (1939), I wrote: "I venture to state that many, many years may pass before anything comparable to this is repeated." Little did I dream that just ten years later these "unparalleled" flights would be wholly eclipsed, *in one day!*

Saturday, October 7, 1939

Bright, with light to moderate northerly winds; 72° average. Swarms of warblers all morning, and a conspicuous flight of blue jays. Some 45 visitors were treated to an unprecedented flight of sharp-shins. The little *Accipiters* began coming in numbers about 8:45, on both sides of the ridge. During the afternoon, however, with increasing wind, nearly all the birds kept to the north slope. Sometimes 15 or 20 sharp-shins were in sight at once about the Lookout. As far as could be determined 60 per cent were adults. Throughout the day the birds flew low, the majority well within range of gunshot. The day's count of 1,872 hawks: 1,658 sharp-shins (635 until noon), 65 Cooper's, 74 red-tails, 14 red-shoulders, 10 broad-wings, 2 golden eagles, 1 bald eagle, 15 marsh, 4 ospreys, 1 peregrine, 2 pigeon and 26 sparrow hawks.

Tuesday, October 2, 1939

Partly cloudy, mild weather, with moderate winds from northwest. The mountain swarming with golden-crowned kinglets—many *thousands* of them, *everywhere;* hermit thrushes also numerous. I wish that all our friends could have witnessed today's marvelous migration of red-tails, and the sight of the golden eagles. Today's passage of red-tails may well be a record-breaker, and the flight as a whole is amazing, in view of the mild weather. The ten species of hawks totaled 1,498 individuals: 2 vultures, 264 sharp-shins, 18 Cooper's, 1,144 red-tails, 59 red-shoulders, 1 rough-leg, 5 golden eagles, 2 marsh, 2 peregrines and 1 sparrow hawk.

Friday, November 3, 1939

Bright, crisp weather, with fresh north wind; 30°-43°. Golden eagles provided a record day! It was an incredible experience when at 12:25 P.M. 4 adult golden eagles rose suddenly over the ridge. A half hour later, another thriller, when a golden eagle and a goshawk drifted toward us, sailing almost side by side. The day's count of 557 hawks included 464 red-tails, 22 red-shoulders, 44 sharp-shins, 2 bald eagles and other hawks, as well as 29 loons. Joseph A. Hagar and Hervey and Frances Elkins, of Massachusetts, were among the joyful watchers.

Monday, October 21, 1940

Unsettled weather with light precipitation until 2 P.M., followed by clearing skies; moderate to fresh northwest winds all day; 32°-42°. About 515 Canada geese in nine flocks passed over the Lookout. One flock of 23 "honkers" passed within 600 feet, and a 24th bird was a *Hutchins's goose,* or at least a small goose exactly half as big as its companions! Two flocks of brant also passed, numbering 31 birds. Many siskins, bluebirds, robins and waxwings throughout the day. Only 190 hawks were tallied to noon. The flight really got under way about 2 o'clock, and continued unabated to 5 P.M. The day's count of 759 hawks included: 2 goshawks, 24 sharp-shins, 5 Cooper's, 705 red-tails (166 until noon), 8 red-shoulders, 6 golden eagles, 2 marsh, 3 peregrines, 1 pigeon and 3 unidentified hawks.

Saturday, September 20, 1941

Bright, with fresh southeast winds during forenoon, almost calm the rest of the day; temperature 70° average. No hawks appeared until 8 o'clock, then broad-wings arrived in large groups, milling high over the "kettle." By 9 o'clock flocks were scattered all over the ridge. We counted 2,232 broad-wings by 10 o'clock, when the flight stopped abruptly, and I guarantee that some birds passed uncounted! Because of the unfavorable wind conditions, many must have passed un-counted. We also had a good flight of small birds—red-breasted nuthatches, flickers and warblers being most conspicuous, as well as a rather late olive-sided flycatcher. The day's count was 2,340 hawks of seven species: 40 sharp-shins, 7 Cooper's, 1 red-tail, 2,281 broad-wings, 1 bald eagle, 1 marsh and 9 ospreys. A few members of the West Chester (Pa.) Bird Club, and five bird watchers from Elmira, New York, were the fortunate observers of this early morning flight.

Monday, October 19, 1942

Crystal clear, cool weather, with brisk northwest winds; 32°-68°. The best hawk flight of the season (preceded by four days of northeast rain and winds) also brought a heavy flight of crows—more than 2,150 passed the Lookout during the day. The sharp-shin flight at its peak, and red-tails staging their first conspicuous movement.. Today's count of 907 hawks of ten species included 627 sharp-shins (495 until noon), 44 Cooper's, 210 red-tails, 10 red-shoulders, 4 golden eagles, 2 bald eagles, 3 marsh, 1 osprey, 1 pigeon, 2 sparrow and 3 unidentified hawks.

Thursday, September 18, 1947

Clear, with light winds from southeast all morning; almost no wind after 2 o'clock—and very few hawks. Many swifts and waxwings moving, and warblers swarming about the

Lookout. The broad-wing procession began with 4 low-flying birds, at 8:10; during the next two hours we tallied 1,018 birds. No tremendous masses as in other years, but a continuous movement all morning, many "piling up" over the Lookout, to circle on the updraft and gain elevation.

Mrs. Junea Kelley, of Alameda, California, left reluctantly in midafternoon, after four days of excellent hawking. Dr. Elsa G. Allen, of Cornell University, and her friend, Mrs. Francis H. Scheetz, of Philadelphia, made their first visit and they saw nearly a thousand hawks, including three of the eagles. Our record for the day included 2,502 hawks of nine species: 30 sharp-shins, 2 Cooper's, 10 red-tails, 2,440 broad-wings, 5 bald eagles, 1 marsh, 9 ospreys, 1 pigeon and 4 sparrow hawks.

Thursday, September 16, 1948

And now for the miracle day, when the sky was literally darkened by broad-wings, giving us a glimpse of the way it must have been any mid-September day a couple of centuries ago. Some sixth sense forewarned me of this flight! John and Grace Prest, of Wilmington, Delaware, were visiting the Sanctuary. They had a week on their hands, enjoying excellent birding with us. I said to the Prests, "Better hang around until Thurday—*that's* the big day." They hesitated, but departed at last to visit some relatives in New Jersey. You can imagine their chagrin when later they heard all about it.

The morning looked hopeless for good hawking. A dull, sullen sky, and a fresh easterly wind—the worst possible wind for a flight—chilled us in body and spirit. But not for long! At exactly 8 o'clock an adult bald eagle circled above Schaumboch's, followed by 50 broad-wings. Then came a continuous movement of broad-wings, on both sides of the ridge, and at moderate elevations, many of the birds so close we could have hit them with stones. There was nothing remarkable the first two hours—only 1,396 broad-wings, and a sprinkling of ospreys and sharp-shins. An additional 1,371 broad-wings were tallied in the next hour. But soon after 11 o'clock a swirling mass of broad-wings boiled over the mountain, and they soon filled the southern sky in a seemingly interminable, densely straggling line, moving rapidly. My 18-power binocular revealed a level sheet of moving birds as far to the south as I could see. It was impossible to count, and I found myself making estimates, for the first time in all my years at Hawk Mountain. My tally for that last hour of the morning was 7,587 plus broad-wings. My companions on the Lookout, making independent counts, found my figures extremely conservative. Many more birds went by. The handful of observers who were present are not likely to see such a sight again. In the more than 7,200 hours that I have watched birds atop Hawk Mountain, there has never been anything remotely comparable to this avalanche of hawks. In that one hour before high noon, we saw more broad-wings than we usually see in an entire season. Only a thousand odd hawks passed the rest of the day; and the day's count was 11,392 plus hawks. This historic migration was witnessed by Donald Bieber and Walter Listman, both of Rochester, New York, Theodore Hake of York, Pennsylvania, Mabel and Ralph Lutz of Philadelphia, and my wife.

Apparently the broad-wings had been pent-up somewhere along the ridge. But why? During the five days prior to this mass exodus, the weather had been favorable for migration, and indeed the collective broad-wing count for September 11th to 15th was 1,530 birds. In any event the birds moved south in a body on this fabulous September 16th. At noon of this same day, George Pyle observed 1,500 plus broad-wings over Riegelsville, along the Delaware River, and about 18 miles south of the nearest part of the ridge. In the days following the 16th we recorded only 1,140 broad-wings.

CHAPTER *14* ## GOLDEN EAGLES AT HAWK MOUNTAIN

"An eagle!" exclaim several boys simultaneously, as a huge, dark bird brings up its sails along the crest of the ridge. More than a score of thrilled spectators are scattered on the rocky promontory, a thousand feet above the valley and overlooking six counties in eastern Pennsylvania. All field glasses are brought into action hastily, and for the nonce nothing else in the world matters but this big bird. Obligingly, it veers in the sunlight, revealing a crown and hind neck suffused with rich, golden-brown. There is hushed silence. As the bird floats out of sight, much animated chatter breaks out among the observers; someone announces that he may at last include the golden eagle in his life-list. Before the day is spent, four more golden eagles are seen.

"I have traveled thousands of miles to see golden eagles, with never any luck until this day," said Professor Herbert H. Beck of Lancaster, Pennsylvania, immense satisfaction oozing from his words. He need never have left his home state to see such avian wonders. Yet, in recent times, the golden eagle has been considered a *rara avis* anywhere in the East.

The majestic golden eagle, "King of Birds," ranges over most parts of the Northern Hemisphere. It was not so many years ago that our American race was associated chiefly with the Far West, as distinctly a part of that region as the prairie

dog and the antelope. In Colonial times, this noble bird occupied the mountainous areas of the East, although it was
never common. Ornithological literature furnishes con-
vincing evidence that the bird formerly nested in the mountainous parts of New England; there are vague reports that it
is still a permanent resident in western North Carolina.

Earl L. Poole, in his brochure *The Birds of Berks County,
Pennsylvania,* published in 1930, recorded the local status of
the golden eagle as: "A very rare straggler in late fall."
Hawk Mountain is in Berks County, and only four years after
Mr. Poole's publication, in our first fall season, when incom-
plete observations were made, we saw an embarrassing number of golden eagles—30 to be exact. The following season,
when daily, systematic observations were begun, we saw 66!
And thereafter the frequent appearance of golden eagles
among the lesser *Raptores* proved to be the most exciting
feature of each season.

Outside of Hawk Mountain circles there were many raised
eyebrows as we reported golden eagles regularly. But seeing
is believing, and rugged individuals who were willing to
perch long hours atop the mountain, in the biting winds of
November, had their doubts quickly dispelled. I shall never
forget a bright, cold morning in mid-November, 1935. Five
or six seasoned observers, among them Earl Poole, had been
scanning the horizons with me. Into our midst came a tall,
genial person who introduced himself as Mr. Spencer; he
had come all the way from Erie to see our eagles. And he was
frankly skeptical.

"Aren't you mistaken about your identification of golden
eagles? According to Chapman's *Handbook,* they're not supposed to occur in the East," our friend suggested with un-
blushing boldness.

"Well," I ventured, with a chuckle, "we do see golden
eagles. Ask Mr. Poole here, he'll tell you. But we always

collect five dollars for each one we produce for doubting Thomases." The words were hardly out of my mouth when two adults appeared, suddenly, almost directly above us. The birds were so close, and their identity so obvious, that the gentleman from Erie was stunned, speechless. How we laughed! Then came a fine view of an immature bird, coasting leisurely down the ridge. When a few hundred feet from the Lookout, it plunged into the woods below us, with legs stretched forward. Finding nothing, it came up, circled several times below our vantage point, affording us one of the best opportunities for study. Mr. Spencer saw five golden eagles that memorable day.

A few days later—and those were the days when the Sanctuary coffers were all too lean—Mrs. Edge wrote to me about Herbert R. Spencer, from Erie, who had written to her most enthusiastically and charmingly about his visit to Hawk Mountain, and with his letter was a contribution of twenty-five dollars, in full payment of five bona fide golden eagles! Nor was that all. Our friend, the proprietor of a metal enameling business, sent us a large shipment of attractive roadside signs, each bearing directional arrows and the spread silhouette of the golden eagle; enough signs to stretch all round the countryside and point the way for other eagle-seekers for years to come.

Of course, I do not wish to give the impression that the golden eagle is a common bird; it is obviously not. But when we began reporting these eagles seasonally, and sometimes in greater numbers than their cousins, the bald eagle, bird people—professional and otherwise—sat up and looked about. Eagles have been getting a much more critical going-over, for in recent years there has been a regular epidemic of these supposedly rare birds throughout the East. Often they show up in the most surprising situations, such as on the north shore of Boston, on Long Island, and even on the Florida

Keys. My wife and I were looking for spoonbills near Bottlepoint Key, in January, 1940, when Bob Allen, of spoonbill
fame, told us quite casually that he had seen a golden eagle
over Bottlepoint only the day before!

At Hawk Mountain I have studied eagles in every plumage, sailing or sweeping past the Lookout at every conceivable
angle. The great birds often favor us with exceptional opportunities for study. They frequently pass obligingly close
to or over the Lookout, provided there is no movement on
the part of the observers. Once, as I sat motionless and par-
tially concealed by a great slab of rock, an adult golden eagle
came within thirty feet of me. Time and time again we have
had the unique experience of looking directly down upon
these birds, within gunshot range. I often shudder when I
contemplate the numbers of these noble birds, and lesser
hawks, that were shot down in the pre-sanctuary days, when
the mountain was overrun with callous, irresponsible
hunters.

Our identifications have been made easily in most instances. The "golden" color of the hind head is seen in immatures as well as in adults. The latter show more or
less gray on their dark backs, and grayish lesser wing-covers
are usually distinct. Young birds are readily identified by the
conspicuous white areas in their wings, and by their white
tails, with *broad, dark terminal bands*—both unfailing characteristics. Eagles approaching in the distance can also be dis-
tinguished, for the noticeably small heads and not too
conspicuous bills of the golden eagles mark those birds from
the huskier-headed, large-billed bald eagles. I might add that
it has always seemed to me that the tail of the golden eagle is
perceptibly longer than, and *not quite so square* as that of
the bald eagle.

After years of study of the flight of both species, I cannot
say with certainty that I can readily distinguish them apart

merely by wing beat, or speed, or the manner in which the wings are held. Occasionally it has struck me that the golden flies more vigorously, not quite so labored as its relative. On rare occasions I have seen both species together over our ridge. A fine opportunity for comparison occurred during the forenoon of November 6, 1946, when a wholly dark adult golden and a wholly dark immature bald appeared together, at moderate elevation. They spent several minutes coasting and circling in unison, and playfully plunging at one another, evidently enjoying each other's high-born, spirited fellowship. After gaining elevation directly above the Lookout, both birds drifted off, side by side, toward the southwest. I noted the longer tail of the golden, and the feathered legs, in contrast to the nearly naked, conspicuously yellow legs of its fellow traveler. But I could see no difference in the length and width or cut of their wings; and in manner of flight they were identical.

It has been my good fortune during twelve fall seasons to see the astonishing number of 1,360 eagles. The drama of this seasonal pageant is all the more heightened when we keep in mind that these "symbols of the wilderness" are found little more than one hundred miles from the Empire State Building! Of course, the figure cited must represent repeats; but it is not to be considered an absolutely complete count, either. Although the daily observations average eight to ten hours, it is a physical impossibility to tabulate every passing hawk, and doubtless many eagles have gone by unrecorded. My count extends from 1934 through 1942, and from 1946 through 1948—the hiatus due to three years spent in the Service. Professor F. J. Trembley, of Lehigh University, was the official custodian and observer at the Sanctuary on week ends during the autumns of 1944 and 1945; he reported the 1945 season as particularly good for eagles, and once saw as many as thirteen golden eagles in one day.

Of the total score, 651 birds (about 48 per cent) were golden eagles. My data for the first six years show an average of 50 per cent of these eagles to be immatures; in the second six-year period the immatures averaged 25 per cent. This is not at all in keeping with the statement of E. H. Forbush, in *Birds of Massachusetts and Other New England States,* that immature golden eagles comprise about 95 per cent of the birds seen—an observation also echoed in Roger T. Peterson's *Field Guide to the Birds.*

Adults and immatures alike appear at Hawk Mountain at regular intervals, usually from early October until early December, with the majority of each season's visitants showing up during the first half of November, when "the wind's like a whetted knife." One or two birds may be seen each September, rarely before the 24th; we have a record of one arrival, an immature, on September 2, 1947, an extremely early bird, and another on September 5, 1942. On many occasions in early November, visitors to the Lookout have been rewarded with the thrilling spectacle of as many as four to nine golden eagles in a few hours, and on at least four memorable dates we have seen as many as thirteen of these grand birds. The 1946 season produced a pluperfect score of 36 birds in one week—literally Golden Eagle Week! The fall of 1939, however, produced our best bumper crop—83 birds.

At this point, the reader may wonder as to the origin of all these golden eagles. Do they drift eastward from the Far West? Perhaps, to a very small degree. My own opinion is that nearly all of the golden eagles that are observed in the East are a remnant of a strictly eastern North American population, and that the birds that frequent Hawk Mountain and adjacent ridges in migration derive from some unknown Northern breeding area. There are few clues to the mystery of this supposed breeding area. But that it does exist is pointed up by a bit of evidence from L. L. Snyder, of the

Royal Ontario Museum, who reports a golden eagle shot in the spring of 1938 by an Indian, while the bird was near its nest, a few miles inland from Cape Henrietta Maria in far-northern Ontario. M. Albert Linton, whose ability to recognize the golden eagle is unquestionable, tells of seeing an adult and a full-grown juvenile learning to fly "somewhere in the Adirondacks" during the summer of 1946. Of the many Eastern occurrences of golden eagles of which I know, an especially interesting one concerns an adult which was banded near Philadelphia in May, 1926, by J. R. Gillin. Exactly seven months later, the bird was killed at Berkeley Springs, West Virginia, which is in the direct line of flight of the southward bound *Raptores* passing over Hawk Mountain.

The golden eagles of the East winter regularly from Pennsylvania south to the southern Appalachians, irregularly or rarely as far north as Labrador. Occasionally in winter I have seen these eagles at Hawk Mountain or near by. An "unusual abundance" of golden eagles in Pennsylvania during the winter of 1927-1928 has been reported by Dr. George M. Sutton. Dr. Walter R. Spofford has recently adduced evidence of a substantial winter population of this species in the "Highland Rim" country of Tennessee.

In their passage over Hawk Mountain, the eagles are sometimes pestered by small fry among the hawks. It is amusing to observe the little sparrow hawks, for instance, make passes at the "lords of the air" with their seven-foot wing-span. I have seen peregrine falcons and even goshawks make thrusts at golden eagles, but always the big birds exhibited complete indifference and a serenity altogether becoming their lordly stature. But there was bound to come an exception to the usual behavior. And it came one afternoon in November, 1946, as if to dispute my answer to a frequently asked question at the Sanctuary, "Do the eagles ever kill anything as they pass?" My answer had always been an emphatic "no!"

Then it happened, in a breath-taking, electrifying moment that makes the occasion as dramatic as anything I have witnessed at Hawk Mountain in my twelve years of stewardship.

Imagine, if you can, lying on your back and gazing with me into the zenith through a pair of 7 x 50 glasses. We see in the field of the binocular a large dark bird, and a small hawk, neither clearly identifiable. We wonder how many hawks have been missed, flying at that incredible height above the Lookout. We switched to the greater reach of an eighteen-power binocular and find that the big bird is an adult golden eagle, its satellite still indeterminate. The smaller bird is making desultory passes at the eagle. Suddenly the eagle thrusts forward, executes an Immelmann turn as effortlessly as a fly landing on a ceiling, and grabs the smaller hawk, which puts up a feeble, momentary struggle. The eagle, with set wings, hurtles earthwards at terrific speed, and, still clutching its prey, disappears into the densely wooded flank of the ridge. The wings of the smaller hawk are fully outstretched during the meteoric descent, and we note the ruddy breast of the red-shouldered hawk. It is all over in a matter of seconds!

I was alone, tense and breathless, and, I must confess, somewhat spent from following closely this hair-raising episode. I felt for the doomed red-shoulder, but, at the same time, I had nothing but admiration for the eagle and its aerial performance. The bird's hunger was far greater, apparently, than its capacity to tolerate any impudence or annoyance. I have seen upwards of 200,000 *Raptores* in passage over the Sanctuary, but this has been the only instance of "big fish eat little fish."

I have spent a good deal of time watching eagles, and have never ceased to be filled with childlike wonder at the great birds. "The way of an eagle in the air" is a vision of inexpressible grace, arousing our deepest poetic instincts and filling us with pure delight. Personally I do not look forward to the day when the secrets of those vast unexplored wildernesses to the far north will be revealed, for their opening will mean the inevitable widespread, indiscriminate use of firearms. Consider the sickening fact of how all wild things have suffered and melted away along the two thousand miles of Alcan highway. Consider, too, the Western ranchers who employ a man to hunt golden eagles with an airplane. Farmers in one state cry for Government help to combat a plague of jack rabbits, while in the next state they kill the eagles which normally keep the rabbits in check. I am afraid the cards are stacked against them, but at Hawk Mountain we will carry on our missionary work, and hope to draw inspiration from the sight of eagles, especially the golden eagles—mystery birds of the East—for a long time to come.

NOVELTIES AND RANDOM OBSERVATIONS

One cannot perch atop a place like Hawk Mountain, days on end, with eyes glued on the skies, and fail to harvest a rich and varied crop of birding experiences. Aside from the seasonal pageant of the hawks, the skies above the Sanctuary have provided us with a good all-round show. From this mountaintop I have had the pleasure and satisfaction of identifying 185 species and sub-species of birds—about 65 per cent of the bird life of Berks County's 920 square miles—which shows what may be achieved on a pin point, so to speak, subjected to close, daily observation during the seasons of migration.

But scanning the skies from the Lookout can also be dismally disappointing. My friends, Mr. and Mrs. H. A. Logan, of Reading, often reprove me because the only birds they saw during their first visit to the Lookout were four crows and three chickadees! I remember a young man from Ohio, a former Air Force pilot, who spent a mercilessly hot week end in the early part of one hawking season—counting only butterflies! Even butterflies may prove interesting, however. Each year in late September I marvel at the migrating hordes of monarchs, drifting lazily over the ridge from north to south.

There are other times in the hawking season—fortunately for us, very rare—when the mountain seems utterly lifeless.

I remember a morning of dead quiet, on October 8, 1947, when, according to my notebooks, "there was no stir of a leaf, no sounds, and no birds except a single golden-crowned kinglet!"

My 7,200 or more hours of hawk-watching have produced countless happy and exciting by-products. I shall never forget a certain quiet afternoon in late October, 1936, when I was alone on duty. A subdued rustle in the low growth in back of me, at one of the lower promontories, caused me to turn round very slowly, in time to see four wild turkeys emerge from the undergrowth and run stealthily over the rocks. I had fine views of the birds. They saw me and flew over to the nearest rock-pile, where three of them scurried away, while the fourth volplaned into the "kettle," a beautiful sight. And a few days later, on a Friday, November 13— just to show that this combination of days can be lucky—a turkey cock sailed in front of me, displaying a magnificent bronze tail as it glided to a near-by promontory and disappeared.

Often, late in the season, when the Lookout is deserted by human visitors, pileated woodpeckers have been my daylong companions. One such day (November 17, 1941) stands out vividly—a brilliant Indian summer day, completely cloudless and windless, with the temperature soaring to 95° in the sun! Only one hawk, an adult red-shoulder, went over. But I was fascinated by a showy male pileated which made a tour of investigation of all the big dead trees about the Lookout. Throughout the day the mountaintop resounded with this bird's wild, piercing, flicker-like cry. Once my eardrums almost burst as the big woodpecker sounded off a mere twenty feet from me.

In September, 1941, a pair of mourning doves nested belatedly at the very crest of the Lookout, successfully rearing two young in a chestnut oak over which many an *Accipiter* zoomed by. And scores of people passed within a few feet of the nest, which I disclosed to no one, until at length the two young doves, for whose safety I was so concerned, "took off" to see the world, on September 13. Could there have been a more fitting symbol of peace at Hawk Mountain!

Sometimes my attention has been distracted from the birds by the presence of four-footed visitors. A fox squirrel startled me on September 5, 1942. I studied it a quarter of an hour or more, as it scampered leisurely over the rocks before taking refuge in the near-by hemlocks. Since the native fox squirrel has been extirpated for forty years or longer, we must assume that our visitor had been introduced in the locality. Hawk Mountain Sanctuary was needed many, many years ago.

Almost any time during the fall, if we are quiet and stir about as little as possible, we may see the red-backed mice and the wood rats which live in the rocky recesses of the Lookout. The rats are disposed to venture from their dens late in the day or in overcast weather. But on many days I have been greatly entertained by the sleek little red-backed mice. One lonely afternoon one of these tiny troglodytes ran back and forth from his cranny, lugging away tidbits which he picked up almost at my feet. Several times the mouse, squatting like a toy image beside the drab rocks, its coppery pelage shining in the unaccustomed sunlight, fixed its bright, beady eyes on mine, for long minutes, as though in appraisal of a fellow-being. I put an apple down for it, and this the mouse nibbled the rest of the afternoon, right under my nose. I also discovered that it was fond of mayonnaise, which it licked from my sandwich wrappings.

Among the lesser mammals I have seen from time to time at the Lookout have been red bats, a locally rare, migratory species. Twice I have seen single individuals in mid-afternoons in October (when they are supposed to be much

farther south) fluttering about the Lookout in their charac-
teristically strong, erratic manner.

I have often spotted deer in the woods below the Lookout,
or along the railroad, or swimming across the inky Schuylkill
at the foot of the mountain. One November afternoon, in
1948, I was jolted out of a deep reverie by a series of strange
sounds issuing from the "kettle." Loud snorting, deep guttural groans, low bellowing, and heavy breathing like wind
rushing before a fire, almost made my hair stand on end.
Then, after much searching of the dense and tangled wood-
land with my binocular, I spied below me, some six hundred
feet distant, a huge eight-point buck, giving four does the
merry-run-around. The buck then herded his golden harem
and demonstrated his mating prowess before my astonished
eyes.

Barn swallows are the curtain raisers of the great fall migrations at Hawk Mountain. We see these birds, joined by
purple martins and other swallows, all apparently migrating,
in early summer. The only book that mentions July migrations of barn swallows, so far as I know, is *Birds Around New
York City,* in which Alan Cruickshank says (page 311)
"Southbound barn swallows are definitely passing through
our region by the middle of July." Hundreds, often many
thousands of the fleeting, graceful birds sweep low over the
Sanctuary woods, in a rather narrow line of flight, every
evening in July and early August. Tommy Hanson and I
counted almost fifty thousand swallows during July evenings
of 1948. These remarkable flights had us mystified until, one
evening in 1949, we discovered the swallows' roosting area,
at Deer Lake, just three and a half miles to the southwest.
There, every July evening, an aggregation of at least fifteen
thousand swallows fills the air like an enormous swarm of
bees.

In late August warblers begin to flood the mountain in waves. One of the most surprising movements of warblers I ever experienced took place on August 26, 1948. The East had panted through the third day of one of the worst heat waves recorded by the weather bureaus. In spite of the sweltering, equatorial conditions, migrant warblers teemed around Schaumboch's. Soon after midday, we counted 54 warblers of 9 species. At the same time, bird watchers in northern New Jersey found their region "almost devoid of birds"—a condition which persisted until September 9th, while at Hawk Mountain we daily witnessed swarms of vireos, warblers, flycatchers and other birds.

Chimney swifts dance across the heavens day after day during the first half of September; I have often counted several thousand in one day. And if hawks are scarce, we may see nighthawks by the hundreds, especially in the late afternoon. Many hummingbirds, in bullet-like passage, zip within inches of us at the Lookout.

Incredible numbers of southward-bound songbirds use our ridge—a super flyway. One of the most tremendous flights I have ever known occurred during the early morning of September 12, 1946. I was up and outdoors an hour before daybreak. The mountain was flooded by full moonlight. As I walked up the road, the cries and twitterings of birds came from all parts of the heavens, and from the woods. The faint calls of three whippoorwills reached me. A great horned owl sounded off, very close, and its deep hooting was acknowledged immediately by a bird about a half mile to the south. The babel of birds in passage continued to pour down from the pale skies for almost an hour after dawn. All that day small birds darted past the Lookout, and in such haste that it was impossible to identify more than a handful. And the day also brought 781 hawks of 8 species.

An historic flight of songbirds was that of September 11,

1948. When in the fog-bound early morning of that day our radio announced the tragic death of countless numbers of "small, greenish-yellow birds" at the Empire State Building, I dashed to the Lookout in time to witness what was the wind-up of a flight of stupendous proportions. In a little more than a half hour I saw thousands of warblers, in small and large groups. The birds streaked past the Lookout just above the treetops, for the most part, but many pitched into the hemlocks and shrubs which crown our vantage point. Most numerous of the hordes of warblers were Cape Mays, then magnolias, and black-throated greens were third in abundance. A Connecticut warbler, a rare bird of low, wet woodlands, climaxed my excitement as it posed for me in the top of a hemlock, within twenty feet. Enormous numbers of small birds were in evidence most early mornings that month.

When migration conditions are favorable, the Lookout is thronged with small birds during early mornings of September and October. In the spring, however, I have found no unusual concentrations there; the birds gravitate to the vicinity of Schaumboch's instead, apparently reaching our headquarters via the edges of the road. I have seen as many as 30 kinds of warblers, and many other songbirds, right at the house.

The abundance of natural food at the Lookout is a great drawing card. Kinglets and warblers find food and cover in the big hemlocks; large gatherings of waxwings often feast on the berries of the mountain ash; juncos, pine siskins and goldfinches exploit the catkins of the black birches; and the fruit of the mountain holly *(Ilex montana)* is devoured by a great variety of birds. Our Lookout might be a rather dull place, I think, from the standpoint of songbirds, were it not for the great clumps of fruit-laden *Ilex*. On September 22, 1946, I saw 3 red-eyed vireos, 2 blue-headed vireos and a Philadelphia vireo all feeding together in one big *Ilex* bush.

And a few days later I counted at least 70 Cape May warblers feasting on, and flitting out of, the same bush. Our mountain holly is really remarkable for the numbers and variety of birds that it has sheltered and sustained. According to the United States Department of Agriculture, the ten *Ilex* species of the United States have been known to provide food for 32 species of birds and other wildlife including deer.[1] I have personally seen 38 kinds of birds (and mice and cave rats) eating the fruit of this one species of *Ilex,* at our lookout![2]

Blue jays migrate regularly along our ridge, some seasons in unusual numbers. They occur from the third week in September until mid-October, in loose flocks, or in orderly processions, on either side of the ridge. I have noticed each season that jays are on the move by 7 A.M., but by mid-afternoon their flights terminate. As a rule, the birds keep just above the treetops, and seldom is there much fuss or noise; indeed, observers at the Lookout must be keenly alert to detect each passing group of jays. At times, an entire group

[1] *Native Woody Plants of the United States,* by William R. Van Dersal, 1938.

[2]
Ruffed grouse	Cape May warbler
Chickadee	Black-throated blue warbler
House wren	Myrtle warbler
Carolina wren	Black-throated green warbler
Catbird	Blackburnian warbler
Robin	Bay-breasted warbler
Hermit thrush	Blackpoll warbler
Olive-backed thrush	Ovenbird
Ruby-crowned kinglet	Wilson's warbler
Cedar waxwing	Chestnut-sided warbler
Blue-headed vireo	Canada warbler
Philadelphia vireo	Redstart
Red-eyed vireo	Summer tanager
Black and white warbler	Scarlet tanager
Tennessee warbler	Rose-breasted grosbeak
Orange-crowned warbler	Indigo bunting
Nashville warbler	Purple finch
Parula warbler	Towhee
Magnolia warbler	White-throated sparrow

will alight on the trees for a moment of rest. It is then that a sharp-shin may appear suddenly and, plunging into the jays, precipitate a confused scramble of flashing blue feathers and a chorus of screams, which may be the signal for the jays to move on. I have never seen a jay fall prey to a sharp-shin. In 1939, the heaviest flight of sharp-shins on record (8,529 individuals) was coincident with the most remarkable flight of jays that I have known, but very little harassing was noticed.

During a sixteen-day period beginning September 24, 1939, I made an approximate count of 7,350 blue jays; and doubtless *many* jays slipped by uncounted. The majority of the birds passed through in a constant stream, regardless of the weather conditions, from September 30th to October 6th. The peak of the jay migration came on October 1st, a day of alternating rain and mist, with raw northerly winds; at least 1,535 jays passed the Lookout, even during the rain, in groups of from 100 to 350. Again on October 3, despite obliterating mists during the forenoon and fresh easterly winds all day, I counted several large flocks at various parts of the Sanctuary, and the far from complete count for the day was 1,250 birds. On October 4th I noticed a curious thing. During the forenoon the "Lookout watch" was taken over by Dr. Harold Axtell of Buffalo, N. Y., while I went down to Drehersville. Standing on the railroad tracks and looking up to the crest of the ridge, I saw (in the space of fifteen minutes) three groups of jays, aggregating 175 birds, leave the ridge and fly due *west* high over Drehersville!

Other observers reported large numbers of blue jays on the adjacent ridges. On our big day, October 1st, Mrs. E. C. Spaide was watching the hawk flights at Point Pelee, and she reported an "enormous" migration of blue jays from early morning until 2 P.M.—more jays than she "ever imagined sojourned in Ontario" (*Jack-pine Warbler,* 1939, page 115).

A scarcity of beechnuts and acorns in the Northern forests may have been one of the factors in this unusual mass movement of blue jays. Or a sudden population increase may have attended an exceptionally favorable breeding season. In any event, it is interesting that this remarkable migration of blue jays, in 1939, was concurrent with the heaviest flight of hawks that we have experienced (22,704 *Raptores* for that season).

Ravens, the largest of the passerines, and among the rarest birds in Pennylvania, have been seen at the Sanctuary, in some instances by large groups of observers, no less than sixteen times since 1934. Most of our ravens have occurred during October, but on September 26, 1947, we saw two of these birds fly past the Lookout. Where do these ravens come from? I haven't the faintest idea. . . .

Ornithologists associate Carolina wrens with low, wet woods. But individuals among birds there will always be, and so it was with two or three Carolinas that spent the entire season of 1947 (late August to mid-November) in the vicinity of the Lookout, where we heard them burst into song frequently, and as late as November 13.

From time to time through the years, I have seen lone snow buntings flitting from rock to rock, and seemingly quite at home at the Lookout. One day in November, 1947, a bunting alighted at the Lookout while 3 Carolina wrens were present—an odd combination! Snow buntings are rare in eastern Pennsylvania. Our ten occurrences of buntings constitute the only records for our region during the present century, so far as I know. When twelve of these rare visitors appeared flying past the Lookout, on October 24, 1947, an unusually early visitation for these waifs from the arctic wastelands, I was as pleased as though I had seen a gyrfalcon. Once during the better part of a day I had the pleasure of watching a fat and bright-eyed little bunting search for seeds among the rocks surrounding me, sometimes within three feet.

When we visit the beaches and coastal waterways we expect to see shore birds, gulls, cormorants and loons. Such birds seem strangely out of place, observed from a mountaintop. Impressive numbers of waterfowl winging through the autumn skies have been an added source of interest and inspiration to observers of the hawk migrations. We have seen 25 kinds of waterfowl in passage over the mountain. The shore birds include large flocks of "peeps," both species of yellow-legs and a flock of 13 red-backed sandpipers—an unusual observation, made on October 17, 1942, by Earl L. Poole and Charles Tracey. Who would think of a Wilson's snipe on a mountaintop! Yet twice early observers have been surprised to see snipe at the Sanctuary: one at our entrance, on November 7, 1935, and again one flashed by the Lookout on October 27, 1940.

Great clamorous wedges of Canada geese and other waterfowl are a frequent and exciting spectacle after the middle of October, coming almost always after a severe storm. Three times competent observers at the Lookout have observed what appeared to be Hutchins's geese, traveling with Canadas: one on October 19, 1936, another on October 31, 1937, and the third on October 21, 1940. One of the most stirring days I can remember was Sunday, November 14, 1948, when throngs of excited observers gazed first at geese, then at high-flying red-tails. The geese, in great, irregular V's, numbered more than 745 birds in 16 flocks—and bright-eyed Tommy Hanson went "loony" spotting Loons "disappear into the sun"—56 of them!

Common loons, like animated crosses, are often seen passing high over the ridge, usually in precipitous flight; as many as 210 loons have been counted on one day, November 11, 1942. In most instances, the waterfowl and gulls fly due north-south, and therefore at right angles to the ridge, which locally has an east-west trend. Only the eagles and hawks and the songbirds follow the course of the ridge. Hawk Mountain is on the direct line of flight between the Finger Lakes and Chesapeake Bay, where most of our waterfowl apparently head.

Loons, I think, are among the most thrilling of birds. Whenever I see them speeding across our sky, toward the Chesapeake, I wish them luck against the hazards of our oil-daubed coasts. Again, in April and early May, I see flocks of loons passing northwards over the Sanctuary. And occasionally we see loons that seem much confused. In September, 1941, five loons headed northwards over the Lookout! Perhaps it was the balmy summer weather we enjoyed all that month that influenced the birds to return north. . . . Four red-throated loons were literally "in a fog" the early morning of October 8, 1939; misty, lowering weather prevailed when these loons loomed up suddenly, only a stone's throw from the Lookout, coming toward us on a level with our position, only a few feet over the treetops.

Five occurrences of brant at Hawk Mountain are noteworthy, inasmuch as this species is rarely recorded away from coastal areas, or off the main paths of migration, and the species is purely accidental in Berks County. I experienced a spectacular brant visitation in the mid-afternoon of November 9, 1938. Some 225 of these birds came out of the north in a compact, formless mass, and passed directly over me in a faintly audible wave of swishing wings.

Snow geese are almost unknown in Pennsylvania, so that our two records for the Sanctuary are of special interest: a loose flock of 9 birds on October 12, 1936; and 26 birds in the late afternoon of October 30, 1938. The latter created much excitement in a large gathering of observers who had had a poor day for hawks. This flock of "wavies" was low-flying and exceedingly noisy. The birds were in such loose formation that five became dissociated from the main group and, cackling lustily, continued southward scarcely more than 150 feet above the treetops, directly over the entrance to the Sanctuary, where I happened to see them.

What could be more bewitching than whistling swans in flight? The few V-shaped flocks of swans we have seen in passage over Hawk Mountain have been among the most thrilling and most treasured experiences of my life, notwithstanding the thousands of swans I have enjoyed studying and photographing at Lake Mattamuskeet, in North Carolina, where many of the birds spend the winter. Our most recent, and most spectacular visitation of swans, came on Armistice Day, 1948. A dozen keen bird enthusiasts were on hand, anxiously scanning the cloudless, windless sky toward the northeast, from whence came only a trickle of hawks. Just before noon we saw a great white wedge move ethereally across the sky, followed by a smaller wedge; and a few moments later, another big wedge, directly over the Lookout, gleaming white in the sunlight, and etched across the deep blue of the zenith. There was not a murmur in the group of observers, for we were spellbound. But our hearts surely sang with joy to see this "flight of swans in fluent script, write singing psalms across the sky," to quote Mrs. Edge. The three flocks of at least 360 birds were sweeping down the heavens to Chesapeake Bay, on the last lap of their long journey from beyond the Arctic Circle.

THE PRESS AND HAWK MOUNTAIN

CHAPTER 16

"If you were a hawk, winging your lofty way over the Blue Mountains, you'd be a sensation. You'd be stared at, pointed at, and clicked at, and there isn't a bird in a gilded cage that could ever stir up so much excitement. For this is Hawk Mountain—*your sanctuary*—and if you swoop down a little lower . . . you would probably blink in amazement at your human audience. In plain words, feathered outlaw, you're as safe here as a sparrow, and there isn't a hunter who would dare shoot you down!" So began a lengthy feature article in the Reading *Eagle,* back in September, 1939. Quite flattering, from a hawk's point of view, but if I were a hawk, I'd resent that "feathered outlaw" stuff! If only people would realize that all hawks, as birds, are a huge success, and just as important and necessary as any other birds.

Hawk Mountain has enjoyed a tremendous amount of publicity in newspapers and magazines. A half dozen recent books have also devoted whole pages, even chapters, to our Sanctuary. Most of this publicity has been highly favorable; some of it has been amusing; and just a little has been plain nasty. A good many of the well-intentioned publicizers of the Sanctuary, apparently awed by something new under the sun—"the world's first sanctuary for birds of prey"—and not quite sure whether hawks in general were worth their salt, have dubbed the Sanctuary with such descriptive phrases as

Predators' Paradise, Killer Haven, or Refuge for Feathered Outlaws. Most people simply cannot throw off the old mental yokes and shibboleths with which hawks as a class have been identified. Typical of the way many feature writers have begun their effusions about the Sanctuary is this from an article in *Holiday* (Preview edition of 1945): "The hawk is a bird of prey, but in Southeastern Pennsylvania there is a Sanctuary where these feathered killers are protected from human hunters. . . ."

A leading article in the fashionable sporting magazine *Spur* (February, 1939) expressed rather ably what many other publications managed to convey but feebly. "The astonishing idea of a refuge for birds of prey" was evaluated as a "symptom" of the changing scale of values of our times. The author, Everitt MacKenzie, himself entertaining no gentle feelings toward hawks, nevertheless, like a true sportsman, presented an unbiased picture, giving credit where credit was due, and he aided the cause of conservation with an accurate, intelligent summary of the economic and biological significance of birds of prey. And he had this to say of the Sanctuary: ". . . a phenomenon which was at its height in May of the past year [1939], when there was incorporated in Pennsylvania an organization called the Hawk Mountain Sanctuary Association, founded for the protection and preservation of American birds of prey. To the reputed sportsmen of the old type, who at a bare thought raised his gun in righteous indignation against the predatory tribes of the air, nothing could be more preposterous or extreme in its sentimentality than the establishment of a place where killers may find refuge. But today one of the most striking manifestations of the change is the endorsement of the selfsame project by leading sportsmen throughout the country."

The "endorsement" was traceable, in part, to the Pennsylvania Game Commission, which, through its widely read

Game News (November, 1936) broadcast these heartening words: "Much good has been accomplished through the establishment of the Hawk Mountain Sanctuary. . . . The editor surveyed the area and found that hunters who formerly slaughtered thousands of these birds, many of them beneficial . . . are now using the sanctuary as an observation post to study their characteristics. Sportsmen and others are urged to visit this excellent bird observation point." The Game Commission, once utterly indifferent to the plight of the raptorial birds, could not have paid us a better compliment. Exactly seven months after this sincere expression of good will, the Game Commission boldly overhauled its antiquated legal code as applied to hawks and provided legal protection to all but the three accipitrine species. This certainly helped our cause tremendously, even if it did little, actually, to help all the hawks.

Amusing sidelights on the Sanctuary, much of it unconscious, have poured from the press. The Philadelphia *Bulletin* urged its readers to visit the Sanctuary, one of the "oddities of nature." The Harrisburg *Patriot* wrote glowingly, adding this interesting observation: "The valley floor, almost under the lookout rocks, is 1000 feet below, so far that a horse and wagon looks no larger than a cockroach." A feature article in a Sunday edition of the Reading *Eagle* wound up with this flight of fancy: "And so, the hawks continue on their journey along the Appalachian ridge, unmolested and free to flap their wings in joyous flight. Perhaps they resent the human eye prying into their feathered glory and invading their Sanctuary with cameras and field glasses, but swooping down to see what it's all about they probably feel that it's much better than looking into a muzzle of a shotgun."

A writer for the Pottsville *Journal* had a terrible time trying to explain (in a lengthy editorial) what it was all about:

"Hawk Sanctuary, on the Blue Mountain near Drehersville, is the first Sanctuary ever to have been established for hawks. This musing must confess to never having visited the Sanctuary, though we have seen its famous Hawk Crag from miles away and have a pretty fair idea of what it's like. It is an immense thing of lichen-blotched boulders, said to have a sheer cliff of 3000 feet. . . .

"Perhaps the most interesting item regarding the flyway is that the birds merely follow a groove on the earth's surface, for the very practical purpose of taking advantage of updrafts which enable them to soar with little effort. But why do the birds fly so low near the crag? The explanation is found in air currents. It is noticeable that the very thing which forms the cliff is a dip in the crest of the mountain. The updraft, therefore, is less as the crag is approached. It is a break in the set order which produces a down-current that pulls the birds close to the rocks. They cannot help themselves, the strongest of them, for they are pulled toward the crag by an abatement of the updraft which may be a downdraft. That is the reason the birds can be observed so well from the Sanctuary." This drafty proposition surely takes the cake for newspaper ornithology.

Girard, the sympathetic columnist of the Philadelphia *Inquirer,* gave us much excellent publicity, for which we have always been grateful, but his information was often sadly distorted, as when he wrote, back in 1936: "Indications are that Hawk Mountain has produced this summer a banner crop of big birds. It has been estimated that 25,000 eagles and their various hawk cousins visit Hawk Mountain in a year. There they rear their young and there they form the best big wild bird show in America." Such information brought scores of sightseers, but it also established an absurd legend, which persists like sin, that hawks are raised wholesale on our mountain, and that periodically the birds spread as far as Philadelphia!

In the winter of 1947 several Rod and Gun Clubs of the Philadelphia area, itching for more targets, began a great squawk about hawks in the local newspapers. They agitated for the annihilation of "hawks flying in bands of as many as fifty upon flocks of songbirds." The would-be hawk-eliminators further insisted that they were "being overrun by hawks which have been permitted to breed in droves at Hawk Mountain." Fortunately for the handful of hawks in the Philadelphia area, this silly campaign was squelched by an army of enlightened bird students and conservationists. Nevertheless, there will probably always be bemuddled and benighted Nimrods who think that Hawk Mountain is a propagation center for hawks.

This fantastic notion of the Sanctuary being a hawk-breeding center even spread to England! In the late summer of 1940, I received the following letter:

Dear Mr. Broun:

I have seen in the May 2, 1940 issue of *The Christian Science Monitor* a striking article entitled *Hawks Protected*. . . .

I am the London correspondent of a chain of overseas papers and often write and publish illustrated articles on natural historical subjects. . . . I am just about to write and publish an illustrated article on your Hawk Sanctuary and should like to ask you, kindly send me a nice series of photos showing the Sanctuary itself, the "private life" of the hawks, their nests, as the littles are cared for by their parents, how they are fed, kept, cured, etc., together with some informative material that would serve as a basis for my article.

I promise to send you copies of my published work that

would undoubtedly mean a great publicity for you and for your Sanctuary.

Yours faithfully,

Signed: M———— L————

Foreign Correspondent,

London, England.

My correspondent heard from me, with authentic information (I practically wrote his article!) and I presume that he was greatly disappointed.

Hawk Mountain Sanctuary was still in its swaddling clothes when it achieved unexpected nationwide publicity through the medium of a long editorial in a popular sporting magazine. The editor of the magazine made a great fuss over "the world's first sanctuary for birds of prey," pooh-poohing the newly-formed Sanctuary, deriding all people who defend hawks, execrating all hawks and extolling rabbits; he confessed to his readers that he had a notion that the beneficial hawks and owls would not be considered so beneficial if it became known that the rabbit was one of their principal items of food. I wrote to the editor suggesting that all conscientious sportsmen who will not hesitate to kill hawks be sent to Australia to help rid that continent of the plague of rabbits, introduced by erring man. The rabbits, propagating by the tens of millions, with no natural enemies to hold them in check, were obviously the answer to the rabbit-hunter's prayers. But it was also Australia's No. 1 headache, to the tune of millions of dollars of property damage. That editor, like certain other exponents of the shotgun fraternity, considered us a pack of witless sentimentalists.

The attitude of the magazine editor was as nothing compared with that of a certain reporter-columnist of a local newspaper. This columnist has often reflected the feelings of a small element of die-hards among the hunters of a near-by county, to whom the Sanctuary and all it represents is anathema. Mention of the Sanctuary in the presence of some of these men makes them boil over. So far as I have been able to determine from this man's column, the fields and streams were created expressly for hunters, human hunters let it be understood, and all creatures who trespass, such as hawks, owls, foxes and other indigenous members of our fauna, are "vermin" which must be killed.

With tongue in cheek, no doubt, the columnist once reported that a hundred or more pigeons had been wing-clipped on Hawk Mountain so they could not fly, and released to feed the hawks, which came diving down to rip apart the helpless victims. Such a practice, he suggested, was something for the S. P. C. A. to look into. He further hinted that the admission fees which we collect from sightseers were used to purchase the pigeons. Since Hawk Mountain had been receiving much favorable publicity, our columnist felt that the full story should be told, in order to acquaint people with the cruel side of the hawks.

Such malicious nonsense was a little too much for even our philosophic stomachs. At a meeting of the Board of Directors of the Sanctuary, it was decided to have our lawyer demand an immediate retraction, or else the columnist was to face prosecution for libel. The reporter promptly headed his column with a statement retracting what he so shamelessly allowed to be printed, but the remainder of his long column contained a diatribe of the most vehement sort, against all hawks, which he classified as murderers—even when they killed mice. Our hawk-hater wrote that he would continue to shoot all hawks. For him the only good hawk was a dead one. Now what can you do with a fellow like that!

EPILOGUE

Hawk Mountain Sanctuary is a unique project. But this project, now in its fifteenth year, has been no picnic, for from the very start it has been like building something tangible out of gossamer. Looking backward from what we hope is solid ground, we have the satisfaction of knowing that our institution has benefited the community immeasurably; that we have thrown some light in dark corners, both at home and far afield; that countless wild creatures continue to live and thrive through our efforts; and that Hawk Mountain has brought pleasure and uplift to many hundreds of people, both young and old. Had nothing else been accomplished, the Sanctuary has more than fulfilled its purpose. Our labors have been justified.

INDEX